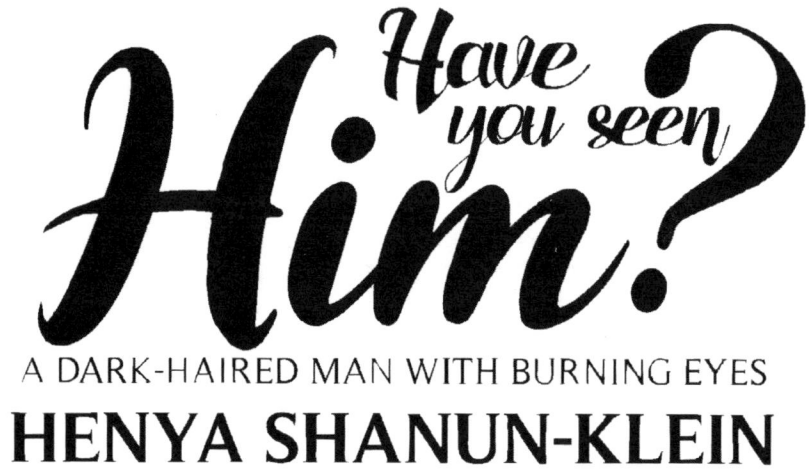

## A DARK-HAIRED MAN WITH BURNING EYES

# HENYA SHANUN-KLEIN

2022

Altman Innovation Products and Publishing LLC

Cape Coral, Florida

HENYA SHANUN-KLEIN, PhD, FT
www.gilis-place.com
drhenyask@gmail.com

Altman Innovation Products and Publishing
346 Bayshore Drive
Cape Coral, Florida 33904
AltmanInnovation.org

ISBN (Print) — 978-1-66784-465-7

ISBN (eBook) — 978-1-66784-466-4

Library of Congress Control Number: 2022909346

Printed in the United States of America

# DEDICATION

**To the Living:** First and foremost, to my beloved son, Shai, and my granddaughters, Jessica and Mika—I love you more than life.

**To the Dead:** To my beloved daughter, Gili—my heart and soul; to my parents, Adel (Adela) and Izak; to my husband, Norman Kagan; to my extended family—grandparents and other relatives murdered by the Nazi.

**Special gratitude:** To my creative and dear friend Michael Altman, who inspired me on my journey to write this edition of "Have you seen Him?"

# FOREWORD

This novel is a story about a journey of faith and love during World War II. Adel and her husband Itchale escaped Poland during the Nazi occupation and traveled to Lviv (Lvov in Russian) in Ukraine. They came to Lviv with nothing but a suitcase and hope for a better life.

Itchale went looking for work every day in order to provide food and shelter for Adel in this tough time during the war. During this time, Russians began kidnapping young men for their war effort. Itchale was caught during this terrible time of kidnappings and suddenly disappeared.

The journey then begins with Adel traveling mostly by foot and train 12,000 miles (approximately 20,000 kilometers) through several countries searching for her husband, who was kidnapped. This is a story about a "woman of valor" Adel, who crosses two continents - Europe and Asia in search of her true love. Throughout the story you can feel their souls yearning to see one another again.

Now we fast-forward eighty years after WW II and history has repeated itself when Russia decided to invade Ukraine. There are many women and children leaving Ukraine into Poland to escape the Russian oppression and war leaving behind their husbands to fight to protect their country.

I can only imagine how many women feel the same way Adel did when her husband was kidnapped by the Russians during the war, not knowing if he was still alive.

Dr. Henya Shanun-Klein is a brilliant author who portrays this story in a factual way with a sense of faith and love.

— Michael Altman
Chairman-CEO Flying Doctors of America
*CEO, Altman Innovation Products and Publishing*

# BACKGROUND

This is definitely not your usual love triumphs over all obstacles kind of novel. Rather, Dr. Henya Shanun-Klein has captured the pathos of the protagonist, Adel, from birth through her life's journey to what seems the ends of the earth to find and bring back the love of her life, her husband Itchale.

During the late 1930s, as war was upon Europe, the Soviet Red Army purged the shtetls of young Jewish boys. Caught up in this terrible happening was Adel's new bridegroom. Dr. Shanun-Klein masterfully weaves the true facts of this story into an incredible Eurasia geographic travelogue, the likes of which, if the story was not factual, one would surmise it was fiction.

Somehow, the author has uniquely employed her own life experiences, including those of being a psychologist and thanatologist (study of death, dying, and bereavement), to provide the reader with a greater sense of empathy for Adel, than an author without her unique background might otherwise produce.

It is not only the wonderment of this story but the author's unique ability to bring to the reader excruciating details of the protagonist's challenges on her journey. She moves the reader from words on a page to literally being in the scene with Adel feeling the grayness of the times, but more importantly feeling her boundless spirit of faith and determination to conquer the evil about her.

Move over Don Quixote, for this is not a story of imagination but of a young woman through insurmountable travails, who literally "did climb every mountain and ford every stream" as those lyrics from *The Sound of Music* regale.

Dr. Shanun-Klein, thank you for allowing the reader to transform the words on a page into vivid pictures of perseverance and for providing us a real page-turner!

—Alvin L. Zimmerman
*Attorney, Former Judge Harris County, Texas*

# ONLY THE DEAD DON'T DIE

Only they are left me, they are faithful still
whom death's sharpest knife can no longer kill.

At the turn of the highway, at the close of the day,
they silently surround me, they quietly go my way.

A true pact is ours, a tie time cannot dissever.
Only what I have lost is what I possess forever.

*My Dead* (Ra'hel, Flowers of Perhaps, R. Friend & S. Sandbank, trans., London: Menard Press, 1995).

# TABLE OF CONTENTS

# PREFACE
## A love that has no boundaries

This book is inspired by the true story of Adel, a young woman who crossed an uncharted land of almost 20,000 kilometers, spanning two continents, from Poland all the way to Russia's Far East and back, in search of her husband Itchale, who disappeared during World Word II.

Itchale (Izak)

Henya-Shanun-Klein(author) and Adel

1946 Refugee camp, Hofgeismar, Germany

# ADEL & IZAK'S JOURNEY

# ADEL & IZAK'S JOURNEY

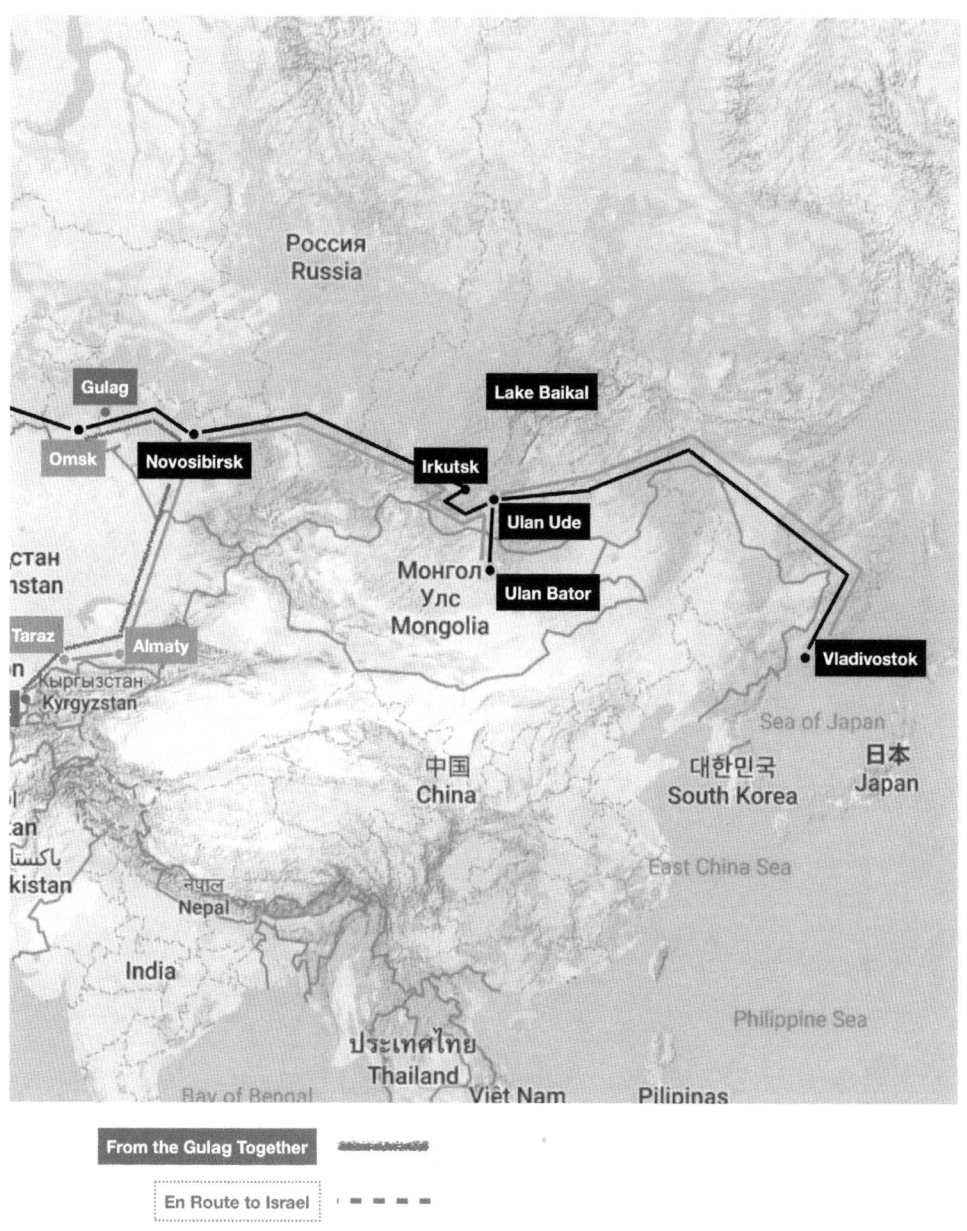

**Map of Adel's Journey**
**Created by Adel and Izak's**
**Grandson and Jessica's father, Shai**

# ADEL & IZAK'S JOURNEY

**Illustrations of Adel and Izak (Itchale) by**

**their Great-Granddaughter, Jessica**

# THE START OF
# A NEW LIFE

# 1

# The Disappearance

"If I don't come back, I want you to take good care of yourself," said Itchale to his wife, Adel, before he left.

An arctic wind howling through the single window cracks of their cellar apartment carried no promise, yet again, for a sunny day.

It was dark outside, and Itchale was ready to go to the bazaar. Adel was curled up in bed. She heard every word but pretended to be asleep. For a change, she did not want the day to begin.

The night before, the young couple had discussed their meager situation. They were facing starvation if they do not find work fast. Meanwhile, they had the down blanket they had brought with them from Poland. It could have come in handy in those cold days, but they had to eat. They could sell it and get something for it that would help them survive a few more days. They had heard the Russians paid well for down from Poland. There were no scissors in sight. Adel used a knife to cut the blanket into pieces. She put them into a basket for Itchale to sell at the bazaar the next morning. That was their plan.

Adel and Itchale were newlyweds in their twenties. Instead of celebrating their honeymoon, they were on the run for their lives as escapees from the Nazis. Polish Jews, illegal refugees in Russia.

They had escaped from Izbica, Poland, to Lviv, Ukraine, hoping to live safely near Itchale's elder brother and sister. But, a few days after their arrival, they heard Jews were being abducted from the streets of Lvov by Russians and sent to labor camps. The couple's worst fear was to be separated.

However, constant fear becomes part of the fabric of life. Under such circumstances, even a daily routine can create an illusion of calmness.

On any other day of the week, Adel would get up before Itchale. She would slip out of bed quietly so as not to wake him. Men need their sleep more than women do, she believed. The same rebellious lock of hair tickled her face every

morning. "I need to do something about it. If I only had a pair of scissors, I would have chopped off this long hair of mine. It would be easier to comb it anyway," she mumbled while brushing her hair with her fingers. She splashed cold water on her face from the leaking faucet in the kitchenette. A quick brush of her teeth woke her up completely.

Since their arrival in Lviv, a month earlier, she had noticed her gums were bleeding. *Not a good sign*, she thought. A gentle massage of her aching gums with her finger was all she could do. Two steps and she was at Itchale's bedside. Afraid to startle him, she lightly touched his shoulder. He usually got up at once. He was not in a talkative mood until he had his first cigarette.

Unless it was a snowy day, Adel would open the single window—to let in some fresh air.

Gray was the ruling color in the cellar. The dark gray concrete floor competed with the stained gray of the walls. To subdue the gray, Adel hung her colorful head kerchief on the window instead of a curtain—to bring some color into the room and for privacy, which was important to her although no one was peeking. All they could see from the window were the legs of people walking by in the street above. Intimacy, she believed, should be kept where it belongs—inside. No need to put it on display.

While Adel fussed around straightening the room, Itchale took his first smoke at the open window. One disapproving look from Adel would send him outside. Even before Itchale finished his first cigarette, she smoothed the grass mattress with one swipe and neatly folded the worn-out blanket—a contribution of a kind neighbor. There was no need to fluff pillows because there were none. Leaning on their arms to sleep served that purpose. The narrow bed enabled sleeping comfortably in only one position anyway—spooning. By the time Itchale finished smoking, a cup of boiled water and a slice of bread were waiting for him on a small table. There was room for one chair. It was not often they could afford a cup of tea, a bowl of soup, or a slice of bread with butter. If there was any bread left, Adel would eat too. If not, she would drink more water. Such days were scant still.

On that Tuesday morning, still in bed, Adel felt as if ice ran in her veins when she heard Itchale say, "If I don't come back—"

"What did you mean? Why wouldn't you come back?"

She sat up, her bare feet on the floor, her back erect, ready to face whatever was coming. With one hand, she removed the defiant lock from her face while with the other she straightened her nightgown. The freezing floor grounded her while sending shivers along her spine.

"Why? What have you heard? Have you heard of any abductions?"

"No, I haven't."

"Do you have a bad feeling? God forbid!"

He avoided her eyes. *She can read me like an open book,* he thought.

He did not want her to worry.

By the door, ready to leave, he said, "No, I don't have a bad feeling."

Adel walked over to him. He loved the smell of her warm body. He touched her arm softly.

"Go back to bed, you'll catch a cold. I wish I could curl up with you."

Adel blushed at the slightest hint of intimacy. There was no need for "mooching and smooching" between them. She knew from the look in his eyes, by the tone of his voice, and by his touch the intensity of his caring for her. Izak—or Itchale, his endearing nickname—knew the depth of her love for him. They were newlywed, but their love for each other, they felt, was ancient. Itchale and Adel, therefore, needed very few words to express their thoughts and feelings for each other.

"It's nothing," he said. "I'll be back soon."

Adel was in tears. "Please stay. Don't go today. We'll find work tomorrow. We'll sell the stupid blanket another day. Not today."

He looked away, avoiding her tears, believing it was his responsibility to be the provider and protector. He hated to feel helpless, not to be able to provide for her or assure her that nothing would happen to him in the streets. These were dangerous times after all. In selling the down blanket, he saw an opportunity to save them from another day of hunger. He felt he had to ignore the rumors about abductions, his foreboding feeling, and Adel's tears. He was convinced there was no other choice. Izak opened the door and walked out.

Only a minute later that felt like an eternity, and still in her cotton nightgown and bare feet, Adel ran after him, trying to stop him. But it was too late. The dark and quiet street swallowed the man and without even a burp.

She ran back to their apartment. The wind slammed the door behind her. If she could only turn back time.

# 2
# One Foot in Front of the Other

She heard footsteps. *Had he changed his mind?* The footsteps faded away. Nothing was going to happen, she said to herself. Itchale will sell the down blanket and bring home fresh bread or eggs. I will cook a good meal from whatever he brings home. I know how to make something from nothing.

She could not go back to sleep. His last words kept churning in her guts. "If I do not come back—take good care of yourself!"

"I must do something," she heard herself saying.

She was cold and anxious. Her teeth were chattering and her bare feet numb. There was no stove in the room, only a kerosene burner to heat up water or cook when there was something available. It felt like living in an ice cube, but it was still better than being outside. She took a sip of the hot water she had prepared for Itchale and a bite of stale bread left from yesterday.

She had to get dressed first. All her clothes were laid on the floor in one corner of the room and folded in two neat piles. In one pile, she kept their wedding clothes: Itchale's dark brown suit, elegant tie, white shirt, and his shiny brown shoes. He wore his wedding brimmed hat daily now. It warmed him and made him look more mature and respectable.

Wrapped in thin paper were a white silk slip, her pure and simple wedding dress, and a pair of elegant shoes with nylon socks folded, one sock in each shoe, keeping its shape. That pile was a bittersweet reminder of a promise for better days. In the second pile were his and her underwear, two woolen dresses, one in navy blue and the other in brown, a pair of woolen trousers, four pairs of cotton socks, a pair of leather boots, a thick blue scarf, and one black glove. The other one was left to "wave good-bye" to refugees on their escape route from Poland. Adel's winter jacket hung on a nail at the left side of the door.

Adel put on the blue dress, two pairs of socks, and the boots.

To take her mind off the terrifying thoughts, she retreated to what she usually did—cleaning and cooking. Since there was nothing to cook, she started cleaning. She took a broom and a bucket, filled it up with water, and started wiping the concrete floor in silence. In happier times, Adel would sing and prance with the bucket in hand while cleaning. However, that day, she struggled not to let out a cry. The only sound was the whish-whoosh of the broom rubbing the floor; the splashing water and the metallic rattle of the iron bucket kicked around the room. There was not much to clean, but she kept cleaning anyway. The floor, the window, the door, outside the door, the sidewalk near the door. Then back to the apartment. The kitchenette, the toilet. She had missed a spot. She filled up the bucket with water again. Adel stopped to stretch her aching back. She wiped her sweating brow, sighed, and went back to scrubbing the walls.

"The skin of my hands is peeling off. Isn't it time to stop? What time is it anyway?" she asked aloud.

There was no clock in sight. Even if there had been, she was not confident in reading it correctly. Adel figured the time by the change of light and temperature outside or by the traffic of people walking by their window. She realized it was evening already only when she walked outside her door to swipe the sidewalk in front.

Adel took another drink of water and a bite of bread and sat down to rest on the edge of their bed. She must have dozed off in her clothes. She woke up shivering. She reached out to touch his body. He was not there. Her mind acknowledged that fact as she turned over to his side of the bed. The worn-out blanket was folded neatly, untouched in the corner of the bed.

She sat up at once. "Itchale? Where are you?" she cried.

It was cold and dark in the tiny bedroom. Ominous silence echoed from the footsteps of the drunkards stumbling to their rest for the night. Shadows watched her from the corners with their blind eyes.

Adel looked around. Squinting her eyes, she tried to penetrate the darkness. Her husband was not there. *Itchale? Itchale! Where are you?* Adel was pacing back and forth. *What happened to you?* She opened and closed the door. The freezing wind hissed and pushed her back to the safety of the room. *Where can you be? Have you disappeared again?*

She slumped on the bed, choking on her tears.

"No need to jump to conclusions," she said aloud. "He was only sixteen then. And he did come back for me in spite of the rumors. We got married," she said, almost screaming.

"My heart is telling me that it's different this time!" She kept talking to herself aloud. She needed to hear an assuring voice, even if it was only hers. "I am going to look for him in the streets." "No. Wait for him, Adel. Don't be foolish. He may come home. What if he does not find you? What then?"

She kept pacing in circles. Something had happened to him. *There is a war. Jews are kidnapped from the streets. I am not going to waste any more time,* she thought.

*He should have been home hours ago. I have to go out and look for him. Slow down, Adel. Think. What is there to think? It's time to do! It's still dark outside. Wait until the sun comes out. No, by then it might be too late! What if he lies wounded on a street corner? I have to go now!*

She wrapped the scarf around her neck, put on her jacket, and walked out the door. She headed to the bazaar, zigzagging her way toward the marketplace. She knew her way to the market. She and Itchale would go there often to look for work, to meet friends, or to hear the latest rumors about home in Poland and the war. And when they could, they bought food.

She had to scour the nearby streets. Her anxiety rose with the growing daylight. The NKVD, Stalin's secret policemen, were everywhere—watching familiar and non-familiar faces alike. Ready to send to jail anybody who looked like a "hostile element to Mother Russia." Adel looked around. No one watched her.

A couple of hours passed. It was not going to be a sunny day. She stood on a street corner overlooking the bazaar. The bazaar she knew from previous visits was usually full of life even at such an early hour.

*Something has happened here. Today is different,* she felt.

Vendors avoided each other. There were no greetings. She could smell the sour stench of anxiety that engulfed the entire marketplace.

While she was scanning the marketplace, looking for a familiar face, the hair on her neck stood up—someone was watching her. A policeman.

She fought her instinct to turn around and look. At that moment, she noticed a familiar figure—Nella, a Jewish peddler, whom she had met before on her weekly visits to the bazaar. Nella was a short and stocky woman who looked like a tree trunk but one with unexpected agility. Adel greeted the peddler with a smile of hope. Although not tall herself, she towered over the older woman. Nella saw the police officer as well. "Koif epes, buy something. We are being watched," she whispered in Yiddish. "How about a package of butter?" she asked. "I have fresh butter."

Adel checked an inside pocket of her jacket. Thank God, there were a few rubles left where she had hidden them. Nella could tell Adel had not come to buy anything that day. She was looking for something or, rather, for someone. The two women bonded briefly in a sense of comradery—Polish Jewish refugees in a foreign and hostile land.

"Are you looking for your husband?" the peddler asked the young woman, knowing her answer.

"Yes. Did you see him?"

Nella nodded her head. "I know Izak. I saw him yesterday."

Adel gasped. "Are you sure it was Izak? My Itchale? When did you see him? What did he do? Tell me! What happened?" Adel whispered quickly.

Her teary eyes pleaded and begged for answers. No loud word was uttered. An undesirable ear might hear their conversation, God forbid.

Nella knew Izak from his frequent visits to the bazaar. Like other Jewish refugees, he was looking for work. On that Tuesday, she noticed him trying to sell something. The next thing she saw were two military trucks with soldiers pulling in to the market square. One soldier announced in a loud speaker that all men who signed up for work at the coal mines in Donbass should line up at the trucks. Only a few men walked over voluntarily.

"Izak was not one of them," she said. "I saw a soldier dragging him. He was pushed into a truck."

People ran trying to hide from the soldiers. The soldiers pushed the hunted one by one into the trucks, ignoring the begging and crying of men, women, and children.

Adel asked again, "Are you sure you saw Izak?"

The peddler swore by her children that it was him.

"Do you know of anybody who came back from the coal mines?" She knew in her heart the answer but had to ask anyway.

Nella's pitiful look was her answer. Adel was terrified but not shocked. After all, both she and Itchale had heard the rumors about the abductions of Jews. However, her worst fear had materialized—separation from Itchale.

A tear rolled down her cheek.

She collected herself. *It's not time for crying. I have to find him*, she thought.

"How do I get to Donbass? How far is it from Lvov?"

The peddler had heard Donbass was somewhere in EastUkraine, about one thousand kilometers from Lvov.

"One thousand kilometers!" Adel said aloud. "You could have said a million kilometers or on the moon—it would have been the same for me. Unimaginable."

With her head down, holding back her tears, trying not to draw attention, Adel walked back to their apartment. She opened the door, hoping that a miracle had happened and Itchale was waiting for her. Greeting her with a smile or even being upset with her for not finding her at home.

She imagined him saying, "Where have you been? I was so worried."

And she would say, "You have been worried? Where have you been the whole night? What have you done?" She would emphasize the "you."

However, Itchale was not there. The tiny apartment looked as though life had been sucked out of it. Her heart contracted in pain. Nothing but vast emptiness lay ahead.

Adel collapsed on the bed, letting out a cry. "What happened to him? What should I do? What will happen to me?"

Her whole life came flashing in front of her eyes—all her losses, her upbringing, her love affair with Itchale, even the six years of waiting for him. She thought then that she had lost him forever. Regardless, she never stopped loving him. She reviewed her life events until that very moment.

The day turned into evening. The shadows went back to the corners of the room, waiting to play with her fears. There was nothing else to do.

She took off her clothes and put on her cotton nightgown. She went to sleep hungry.

When she woke up the next day, her face was stained by tears. It was late afternoon already. Shadows crawled on the walls, gathering for the night. The days were short in the winter.

"Enough with daydreaming, Adel," she heard herself say. "Crying will not bring back Itchale. I have to hurry, go out and find him!"

She looked around. Her eyes caressed their bed for the last time. With her fingertips, she gently touched the dent in the bed where Itchale's head used to rest. She pulled down the head kerchief from the window. Gray light stained the shiny glass, making the room once again look dreary and completely vacant of life. "It's time, Adel," she said aloud. "Take only what you need: the few rubles, what's left of the bread, the butter, and the silk slip. Who knows? You may wear it for Itchale one day. Silly thoughts. Leave behind everything else. The neighbors will make good use of it."

She opened the door. It was not too dark.

Slowly and quietly, she closed the door and, without looking back, put one foot in front of the other and started walking.

# 3
# Don't Call Me "Mumme"

Adel was destined to live.

Born in Izbica, a Jewish shtetl, a small town in southeast Poland, toward the end of World War I, she grew up into the Second World War. Her birth was not expected to be a joyous event.

Hersh the widower was Adel's father. He was in his late fifties when Mendl, the shtetl's matchmaker, approached him with a proposal to remarry. He was a father of five, three of them married already, and a grandfather of two.

Well-meaning neighbors described Hersh as a respectable widower. He was tall, blue-eyed, with a nicely trimmed salt-and-pepper beard.

He did not need reading glasses and had good teeth. In short, he was "a good catch." He was also a self-learned, soft-spoken man. Versed in the Torah like most Jews, but unlike many others in the shtetl, he could read not only Hebrew and Yiddish but German, Polish, and Russian as well. He owned an apple orchard and a couple of workhorses. However, he barely made ends meet. There was not a big demand for his apples or luggage to carry by his horses. His children did not go to sleep hungry, but they were not full either. They had just enough to get by.

Mendl the matchmaker was aware of Hersh's meager condition, but it did not deter him. On the contrary, it challenged him. After all, he was known to be "the matchmaker of matchmakers"—the best of the best. While other matchmakers would snoop around the shtetls in their disheveled coats, worn-out shoes, and crooked berets, trying to seal a deal, Mendl rarely ventured out. He would approach somebody with an offer only on occasions when there was an opportunity to make a good deed, or better—a sure success in making a good deal. Parents would knock on Mendl's door asking for his help in finding a good match for their son or daughter. People gossiped that he employed an army of spies that scoured the nearby villages and towns to collect information about potential candidates for matchmaking. Winter or summer, he used to wear a tall fedora hat, an overcoat, and shiny shoes. He was respected for his appearance and knowledge.

"Mendl knows the pedigree of all candidates down to the biblical times of King David," people said.

With Hersh, Mendl saw an opportunity to seal an excellent deal, to make the best of all worlds. On one hand, a mitzvah, a good deed—to have a poor girl marry an established, in age at least, widower—and on the other hand, to make some money in the process.

"Reb Hersh," said Mendl, "make a mitzvah for your children."

He knew how to convince a customer. "They need a mother, and you should not be alone." Hersh, towering over Mendl, listened. He was not offended or surprised by the matchmaker's suggestion. True, he missed the company of a woman. Moreover, the youngest child needed motherly caressing from time to time. He had been widowed for a while, and people were talking. *Perhaps Mendl is right and it is time to start looking*, he thought.

However, he was not in a hurry to say yes or no. Hersh was concerned he might not be able to provide for a new wife and a young one besides.

*She might want a child of her own. Who needs that? At my age? How will I feed another mouth?* he wondered.

But since Mendl bothered to come to his house, out of sheer respect, Hersh asked the matchmaker, "Who do you have in mind?"

"Bela, the Ackerman's eldest daughter," answered the matchmaker.

Hersh knew the family. They were from a nearby village, known for being good people, but unfortunately poor, and for their beautiful daughter Bela. The matchmaker was encouraged by Hersh's question. He interpreted it as a maybe. Therefore, the next day, just after the evening prayer, he invited himself to the Ackerman's house and approached the father with the same proposal. Bela was a blue-eyed, thin, tall, blonde beauty. She had some suitors, but because of her modest ascription, she had few prospects for a good match. She did not expect to fall in love. In the traditional society and the religious family she grew up in, an arranged marriage, with a divorcée or a widower with or without children, was all she could expect. This was true for generations and for all of her poor friends. The few rich ones had choices which Bela could only dream about. At best, she and her parents had hoped to like the man she would marry. Bela knew very well her only dowry was her youth and fleeting beauty.

Mendl's matchmaking went well. In no time, Bela and Hersh were married. Miraculously, they liked each other. She liked his soft talk, his well-behaved children, and the humble but warm household. He liked her respectful and gentle manners. He felt he was blessed once again with a wife and a mother to his youngest children. He was pleased. *A beautiful wife expands a man's mind,* he thought.

However, not joy but "Oy vey, another mouth to feed," was his reaction to the news that Bela was pregnant.

As it turned out, Bela was too young to be a mother to Hersh's children and too weak to survive the delivery of her own baby. She was in her early twenties when she married Hersh and in her midtwenties when she passed away. As the baby girl breached her way into this world, crying, her mother left it—in one long sigh.

Hersh cried silently into his beard. He lamented their bad luck for the sudden death of his young wife, for the newborn who would grow up without a mother, for his orphaned children, and for himself for becoming a widower a second time. The baby girl screamed at the top of her little lungs. Clearly, she wanted to live. Hersh was grief stricken. What should he do? Who could help him?

His three oldest children—two sons with their wives and his oldest daughter and her husband—all came forward and assured their devastated father they would each take turns to raise the baby girl. They did—Zelda, his oldest daughter, in particular.

Death was a common visitor in the shtetl. Zelda knew what to do. She had lost her mother and now her young stepmother. There was no time for crying. She had to attend to the newborn. It had to be bathed and dressed and fed. The baby's screams turned into a whimper, as though mourning the mother she would never know. Zelda imprinted the baby by saying, "Adel was born in a wet spot."

It was a bitter cold night in December on the second candle of Chanukah when Adel was born. It was probably in 1917. World War I was not over yet. Who paid attention to the exact date? No one registered her birth. It was not important when she was born, only the fact she was born. The registration of a Jewish newborn was not a priority on anyone's list. Neither was the death of the newborn's mother. There would be too many questions asked by the registration clerk at Izbica's city hall.

Those were chaotic times, right after the first war and before the deadliest of all wars. The Russians came to Izbica and left, then the Austrians, finally the Germans. Public buildings were destroyed and documents were burned. Life experience which passed from generation to generation taught Jews not to trust authorities in documenting their life events. In order to survive, they had some time to minimize their existence.

She was named Adel by her father. It meant "noble" in German and in Yiddish, "gentle and sensitive." However, her birth name was less meaningful than the nickname she was given by well-meaning mourners in the shtetl. With her mother's death, she was naturally referred to as "the orphan."

Her grieving father was distraught after his wife's death and could not bond with the baby girl. Her mere survival was a painful reminder of his wife's death. He let Zelda and his two older sons care for the baby. The infant was shoved from house to house, from half sister to half brothers and to their wives. They were all busy with their own hardships, but they took care of the orphan as a mitzvah that was expected of them. They fed her when they ate and dressed her the best they could. But no one had the time or energy to play with her, sing her a lullaby, or just hold her close to their hearts. The bereaved father came to visit his baby daughter occasionally. But he never took the little girl, who looked a lot like her mother, into his arms.

From a very young age, Adel was expected to help with household chores. As a result, she matured fast and learned to be self-sufficient.

"She is wise beyond her age," Zelda used to say.

As she was growing up, Adel knew her brothers and sister did their best to take care of her physical needs of food and shelter. But, because of their hardships, they were too worn-out to attend to her emotional needs and give her warmth or empathy. Nevertheless, she did not feel as if anything was missing from her life, except for a mother. That remained like a hole in her heart to her last day.

Adel was only three years old when one of her sisters-in-law told her to pick up her crying baby. The baby was chubby and weighed almost as much as Adel did. When she tried to pick him up, she fell with him still in her arms. The baby screamed and his mother came running. Without asking what happened, she pinched Adel's scrawny arm. Adel felt that emotional pain for years. What hurt her more than the physical pain was the injustice of it. She used to cry in silence. Nobody was around to wipe her tears.

Decades later, Adel described that incident in her journal: "Az ih bin giewein in bai der giter iz mir giewein git, nor ba jena szweigarin hob ih mer giewaint wi gielaht." (When I stayed with the good one [sister-in-law], I felt good. But when I was with the other sister-in-law, I cried more than I laughed.)

When Adel was about four years old, her father passed away. She was orphaned once again.

After their father's death, Zelda remained the main caretaker of the orphan. She raised Adel until she left home with a husband. Zelda was like a mother to her—but not a real mother. She never let Adel call her "mumme" (mother). The little girl tried to call her "mumme" only once. Zelda reacted in anger. "I am your sister, not your mother, and don't you ever forget that!" she yelled, waving a warning finger at the little girl.

Adel never forgot. Her whole life, she envied anyone who had a mother and was privileged to call that person "mother." However, the little orphan had a merciful protector—Zelda's husband. Whenever Zelda yelled at her, her husband would say, "Hush, Zelda, where is your compassion? She is an orphan. It's a sin to hurt an orphan."

Zelda sent Adel to a Catholic elementary school. She was the only Jewish child in her class and possibly in the school. Why was she sent to a Catholic school, twelve kilometers away? Perhaps because it offered a better education? Or she wanted Adel to be disciplined by nuns? Or perhaps she wanted Adel to learn Polish like a gentile, and thus be better prepared for the world outside the shtetl? The seven-year-old child was not aware of her sister's reasoning. She was excited to go to school and could not wait to wear the school uniform—the green-and-blue plaid skirt, the ironed white blouse with the black bow tie, and the navy blue jacket. Even the heavy boots that she had to wear for the long walk, and which ruined the festive look of her uniform, did not bother her. She sang and skipped steps all the way, happy to meet children from nearby villages. It was tough to walk in the snow during the wintertime. But then she would sometimes get a ride by a passing villager.

Adel looked forward to the mornings when Zelda brushed her undisciplined hair into two braids. She even liked it when Zelda dampened a finger with spittle and straightened rebellious locks while scolding her. As if Adel's curly locks indicated some undesirable twist in her character. Adel cherished even those moments.

The Jewish child learned to recite Christian prayers and make the sign of the cross whenever Jesus was mentioned. She loved the school ceremonies, the prayers, and the songs. And if the teachers, the nuns, would not have referred to her as "filthy Jiduvka" (filthy Jewess), she would not have known she was different from the other children. Her classmates, too, encouraged by the nuns, called her by derogatory and hurtful nicknames. That upset her.

One day, she came back from school crying. A teacher, who always addressed her as "filthy Jiduvka," walked over to her seat, and to Adel's horror, pulled a hair out of her head. The teacher showed the hair to the class and sarcastically said, "How dare this Jiduvka has such blonde hair? We should use her hair instead of white sewing threads."

Zelda might or might not have been moved by Adel's crying. However, after the third grade, when Adel was about ten years old, Zelda took her out of school without any notice and sent her to work.

"The orphan knows Polish good enough, and it is too expensive anyway," she explained to her husband.

He agreed. It was too expensive. But more important, as a wise man who valued a peaceful life, he knew better than to argue with his wife.

Adel was sent to work as an apprentice to a seamstress. She learned the trade, but she never liked that work or the seamstress. Being fluent in Polish, she found a part-time job as a clerk in a small office. She grew up to be a beautiful girl who attracted the attention of many in the shtetl. She was quite tall and slim. And with her high cheekbones, wavy blonde hair, and slanted blue-greenish eyes "katzene oigen" (cat's eyes), she looked like a gentile. To her embarrassment, at age twelve her curves started showing. She was usually shy but was not afraid to speak her mind when needed. She was friendly but not chatty. "I speak when I have something to say. Otherwise, I keep silent," she used to say.

Neighbors used to invite the orphan to their homes, to help with their kids. After all, they said, it was a mitzvah. She was particularly welcomed at Henia and Wolf 's home. Henia liked the spirited little girl. She was amazed at her joy of life in spite of the circumstances of her upbringing. The neighbor was delighted to see Itchale, her youngest son, getting along with the girl who was his age.

"Aren't you worried about your son playing with the little girl?" asked neighbors who questioned the mother's wisdom in encouraging the attachment of the two children.

"Itchale is a smart kid, wise beyond his age," said his mother, "but he is restless. This girl calms him down."

Itchale was always ready for an adventure or at least for a good argument with adults or other children. His mother used to tell that "his first word was not 'mumme' but 'nein!' (no)."

At first, the two children played together like siblings. But, gradually, they started withdrawing from the company of other children and created their own private world. They shared their inner thoughts, dreams, and wishes. Their feelings for each other blossomed. They held hands when nobody could see, but they did not dare kiss on the lips. Itchale, bandit that he was, would occasionally surprise her with a kiss on her cheek. They fantasized aloud about getting married when they grew up. Itchale swore his eternal love for Adel. At age twelve, however, "eternity" might be short-lived.

Itchale was good-looking—slim and athletic, with black-raven hair, and piercing green eyes. Some disapproving neighbors described him as "too smart for his own good." Having a mind of his own, he refused to attend a yeshiva, a school for religious studies, and instead went to a secular school. There he met non-observant Zionist youngsters who belonged to a national movement that supported the re-establishment of a Jewish homeland as defined in the Bible. He even started smoking, for heaven's sake. This rebellious behavior was unheard of in those times at the shtetl. "A boy from a good and respected family should attend a yeshiva and not chase girls or Zionists," said the caring neighbors.

When he was about sixteen years old, Itchale, who was versed in Polish newspapers and a few free world books, decided to leave home to study a trade in the big city—Warsaw. The distance between Izbica and Warsaw was only two hundred and forty kilometers, but the cities were a world apart. Itchale did not run away from home. He assured Adel he would come back, although he did not promise when. She understood why he left, but she protested, softly, nevertheless. She knew that once he had made up his mind "only God could change it." He left with his parents' blessing. "If the kid is not Rabbi material," said his father, "then let him become an honest tradesman."

# 4
# One Small Suitcase

Six years passed. Adel was in her twenties and was still waiting for Itchale.

She did not know if he would ever come home to marry her, although she had hope he would.

She had no interest in any of the suitors introduced to her during the years Itchale was in Warsaw. She rejected all the shtetl's matchmakers' attempts to find her a good match, although, as an orphan, her main pedigree was her gentile-like beauty.

She, just like Bela, her deceased mother, came from a "good but unfortunately poor family," as the headshaking matchmakers referred to her. Because of "the orphan's misfortunate status, it was not wise," they said, "to reject such excellent proposals as that of the tailor's 'slightly stammering son' or of the 'recently widowed butcher.' What does she think of herself? Her beauty will fade," said the wise matchmakers. "Unlike her poverty, poor thing. That is here to stay."

Adel heard their tongues clicking "tut-tut" in disapproval. "Who is she waiting for? For the Messiah?" asked the prophetic matchmakers.

Zelda did not know what to think.

She consulted her husband. "Why is she waiting for Itchale? Do you think he promised her something she is not telling us? Ask her. She likes you better than me."

Zelda's husband shook his head. "What do you want of the poor orphan? She is still young."

"Twenty-something is 'still young'?" protested Zelda. "Did you forget? At her age, I was a mother of two already."

"Well, she is different from you," he concluded.

"Or—she is just plain stubborn!" Zelda had to have the last word.

One evening, in the fall of 1939, the fragrance of blooming lilac blended with the smell of war already in the air swirling up a scent of expectancy.

The train from Warsaw pulled into the Izbica station in an asthmatic huffing and puffing. It came to a full halt in a shrieking sound of relief. One door opened. A man got off.

The train from Warsaw to Zamosc passed through Izbica, but it did not stop there too often. When it stopped, it was considered an event worth reporting in the town square. Yunkle, one of the shtetl's bums, who was always at the station, was the self-appointed "reporter." Better there, at the station, than at home with his nagging wife and hungry children. Besides, life was more interesting waiting for something to happen than to make it happen.

The reporter dragged himself closer to take a better look at the man. He could not believe his eyes. It was Izak. Itchale! To be exact, Adel the Orphan's Itchale. The one and only she was waiting for.

People gossiped that he went to Warsaw at age sixteen because he refused to attend a yeshiva. They whispered he worked in Warsaw as a painter. "Can you believe it?" they said. "Painting houses, not canvases. And for that he left the religious life? Poor parents. God have mercy," added the pious souls.

"Izak" was the young man who got off the train, not "Itchale." He shed Itchale when he left Izbica. Or so he thought.

He was about twenty-two years old now, very handsome (men and women agreed), his black-raven hair full and sleek, pulled back to reveal a tall forehead, and green piercing eyes. Tan skinned like his Mediterranean ancestors, head high and a confident stride made him look taller than he was. He even grew a mustache, fashioned after Clark Gable, the renowned Hollywood actor. After all, Izak was not a shtetl boy any longer but a man of the world, a big city man from Warsaw, mind you. He wore a nice jacket with a matching tie and carried a small, brown, leather suitcase. The reporter craned his neck to see if more luggage followed. But no luggage. Only one small brown suitcase that matched Itchale's shiny brown shoes and elegant brown trousers. This was all he brought with him after six years in the big city.

Izak did not notice Yunkle the reporter or anyone else at the train station. He was a man on a mission. He left the station determined to go straight to Zelda's home where Adel lived. He hoped she was still waiting for him, while he knew in his heart that she had.

People whispered, "God in Heaven! Itchale is not going to his parents' house. He is walking to Adel. Who heard of such a thing? But what can be expected of him? He was always a rebel."

Itchale's parents knew he was coming to town. However, he did not write to them why he was coming back. His mother guessed though. She told her husband, "Our Itchale is going to propose to Adel. She has been waiting long enough for him." Her husband nodded in agreement. He always liked his soon-to-be daughter-in-law.

One kilometer and a twenty-minute walk was the distance between him and his parents' home. But one kilometer and six long years separated him still from his soon-to-be betrothed. If she only knew.

From behind closed shutters, dozens of inquisitive eyes watched him as he marched toward Zelda's house, and they asked themselves, "Why is he carrying only one suitcase? What does he have in that suitcase?"

Adel never regretted her decision to wait for Itchale. She agreed with Zelda that she was stubborn. "People may be right. It was probably a bit foolish or even naïve of me to reject all suitors and keep waiting for him," she told Zelda. "But my heart tells me that Itchale will keep his promise to love me for eternity. We have loved each other since we were twelve years old. Why is it difficult to understand that I am waiting for him? He is my 'bashert'! (foreordained spouse, a soulmate, a destiny)."

While Zelda rushed to welcome the approaching guest, Adel hid behind the front door, too shy even to peek through the window. She shook. Her heart raced. *Is he truly coming to see me? What if it is just another rumor, one of many I heard about him during the years? He is a man now.* "With a mustache," the reporter had said. "Like a movie star. Wearing a tie and carrying one small suitcase, with no luggage."

*Will he recognize me? Is he going to stay or has he come for a visit only? Dare I think of what my heart is aching to hear?* She clenched her fists, struggling not to break the door open. She forced herself to stay calm. "Si past nisht." (It was inappropriate to show her eagerness to see him.) She could hear Zelda's scolding.

Adel had no time to change her dress or to comb her hair. A splash of cold water on her flushing face and a quick brush of her thick golden locks with her fingers would have to suffice. *I cannot compete with the big city beauties*, she thought, *even if I wanted to anyway. I am just a simple shtetl girl. But he is coming to me.* For a fleeting moment, a victorious smile replaced her anxiety.

And Itchale? He started his march with a confident and well-aimed strut. However, as he progressed, he became gradually aware of the eyes watching him behind half-closed shutters. In his mind's ear, he could hear the birds spreading new rumors.

Rumors had accompanied him since he could remember. Rumors about his smoking, about his supposedly adventurous life in Warsaw, and more. It used to bother him during his first years in the city. He was afraid vicious rumors would reach his parents and Adel and would hurt them. During the years, there were times he was even amused by being of such interest to people in the shtetl.

There was only so much he could explain in his letters. After a while, the rumors did not bother him any longer, and he stopped writing regularly. Life in the big city was intense, and at the end of the day, he was too tired of telling about his new life to those who lived miles away, in a world different from his.

*How can I begin to explain my new life?* he thought. *What am I? A writer?* This was how he excused himself for not writing.

While walking, he could feel the gentle breeze nudging him forward but at the same time imbuing him with a faint feeling of insecurity. He slowed down and straightened his new tie. He was aware of the dusty road staining his shiny shoes. The road seemed longer than he remembered. With every step forward, he became less confident—less like "Izak" and more like "Itchale."

*What if Adel is not waiting for me? How can I explain the long years of occasional writing? How can I excuse the rumors, especially when some were true?*

Izak did learn to gulp down a shot of vodka or two, spoke Polish fluently and without a Jewish accent, learned Hebrew and Russian and a few other languages. And yes, no denying, in Warsaw, he expanded his horizons and picked up a few polka steps that helped him with the ladies. He definitely enjoyed the company of some gentile beauties from the big city and some from smaller towns. Izak did not check their pedigree. And although he did not live by all of the six hundred and thirteen Jewish commandments, he attended some which enabled him to feel like a Jew still. Occasionally, he went to a synagogue, especially on the High Holidays, mainly out of respect for his parents. He perceived himself as a decent, hardworking, hot-tempered but good-hearted man.

*I love my family of course*, he assured himself. *But I have loved Adel since I was a kid. She is the love of my life, and no Warsaw experience has changed that!*

The dusty road came to an end eventually. And Itchale, not Izak, found himself in front of Zelda's door. As if time had stopped. Everything seemed to be in slow motion. The silence was deafening. On the footstep of Zelda's door, his belief in God was resurrected. Itchale took a deep breath, wiped the dust off his shoes on his pants, and knocked.

God had mercy, and after a time that felt like an eternity, Zelda opened the door and saw him, an elegantly dressed, well-built young man. His green eyes looked straight into hers.

*What the hell? Look at the devil! He is more handsome than I remembered*, Zelda thought. Embarrassed by her thought, and made self-conscious by Izak's gaze, she looked down, averting her eyes.

It was Itchale who straightened his tie again and cleared his throat. But for a brief moment, it was Izak who smiled at her slightly crookedly while twisting the left corner of his mustache. He recognized a woman embarrassed by his masculinity.

Zelda lifted her eyes. *He looks so confident and endearing. His smile is manly and confusing a bit*, she thought, *but it does not fool me. It is boyish still. Anyway, he came for Adel, not for me.*

As if suddenly awakened from a daydream, Zelda pushed the door open and invited him in.

The humble cottage had not changed much in six years. Itchale noticed the walls needed a fresh layer of paint and one shutter hung dangerously from its hinges.

"Where is Adel?"

As if she had read his mind, Adel, golden locks and eyes bluer than the summer sky, burst toward him from behind the door.

Zelda faded away into the shadows of her house. She joined her husband and children who waited politely to greet the guest.

Itchale could not be bothered at that moment with others. Adel was all he could care about. And she was standing right next to him. Finally.

The silence broke at once. One of them mumbled some-thing. Hands touched accidentally, sending tongues of fire into their veins. Shy but inquisitive blue gazes crossed paths with green ones in disbelief. Who can remember what exactly hap-pened in those blurry moments? Adel and Itchale seemed to be under a spell as they stood in the dim hallway. Zelda watched from a distance.

She turned on the lights.

Itchale broke the spell. Without a word, he gestured with his hand to the two women to follow him to the kitchen. With pounding hearts and wide-open eyes, they watched every move of his. As if on stage, Itchale put his suitcase on the kitchen table. In one swift motion, he opened the suitcase: a white wedding dress, simple and pure, lay there, quietly awaiting Adel.

# 5
# Germans on the Riverbank

It fit her like a glove. Adel felt like a lady from Warsaw when she wore the wedding dress.

She bought a pair of fancy leather shoes to match the dress. They were beige and shiny, with a small heel and a delicate ribbon on top. They felt a bit tight on her feet. For the occasion, Zelda pinched Adel's cheeks to make them look rosier and smeared some lipstick on the bride's lips while mumbling, "Look at those lips. And the groom? Huh. Look at his excitement. As if there's no worry in the world."

Zelda's hissing felt like an arrow shot straight into the bubble of her momentary happiness. *Oy Zelda*, Adel thought as she looked at her. *If you only knew how much it hurts.* Her eyes expressed what her mouth could not.

She did not judge her sister though. She understood that sometimes, at the bottom of joy, lurks sadness or jealousy.

Itchale and Adel were engaged the day after he returned from Warsaw. A couple of weeks later, they married. The wedding ceremony was at Zelda's house, modest and short. The guests were all family relatives. The Rabbi said what rabbis say at weddings. And considering the times—the beginning of World War II, shortly after the invasion of Poland by the German army, the Nazi soldiers already on the banks of the river Wieprz, on the outskirts of Izbica— the traditional blessing of "mazel tov" sounded more like an expression of wishful thinking than a belief that good luck awaited the newlyweds.

One morning, taking the scenic route near the river on her way to visit Zelda, Adel saw the most handsome men, all in uniform, blond and tall. "They were shaving. I could smell their shaving cream!" she told Zelda, slightly embarrassed by her admiration.

"You should have seen the Russian soldiers who were here before. Shaving cream was not what smelled from them." They laughed.

"The German soldiers are like snakes that we may be drawn to look at while at the same time be afraid of," Zelda said. She acknowledged the conflict between the appalling and the appealing.

The soldiers' presence on the riverbank was a bad omen.

The air swarmed with rumors. Everyone in the shtetl had an opinion about what was going to happen to the Jews. Those who were old enough to remember World War I or the pogroms, the massacres of Jews in Russia and Poland, predicted another pogrom. Although no one could fathom what the Germans were planning for the Jews, most of the young people agreed time was running out for all.

Uncertainty and fear ruled.

But life is usually stronger than fear. So Adel and Itchale tried to live like a normal newlywed couple. They rented a small apartment not far from Zelda. Itchale went to work as a painter, and Adel was happy to stay at home, cook, clean, and help her in-laws or Zelda, when needed. Itchale was the provider and in charge of paying taxes in the close metropolis of Zamosc.

But fear of the approaching German army was contagious. Everybody in the shtetl talked about escaping to Russia. Adel and Itchale discussed such a possibility as well. Itchale's oldest sister, Etel, and her family, his oldest brother, Azriel, his wife and their two children lived in Lvov, Russia, already. In letters to his parents, Azriel tried to convince them to join him. Adel and Itchale felt helpless when they, too, failed to convince their families to escape.

Wolf, Itchale's father, said, "Unlike the Russians and the Ukrainians who had a reputation for their execution of pogroms, the German people are known for their civility. Our family came to Poland from Germany, and we have lived peacefully with the gentiles for generations, in Izbica alone for hundreds of years. Why then would they want to harm us now?"

The parents, brothers and sisters, and other relatives were determined to stay together in Izbica "until the end." They meant the end of the war.

Before they escaped to Russia, in a patriotic or desperate attempt to protect their families from what seemed to be unavoidable, Izak organized a group of men from the shtetl to join the partisans, the Russian civil resistance movement to the Nazis. It was a group of fighters whose only battle experience was in Talmudic issues or with paint and a brush like Itchale's.

One night, when he thought Adel was asleep, Itchale snuck a gun into their home and hid it under their bed. He was startled when she said, "Itchale, don't you know that men can hide something only when their wives pretend to be asleep? And I am not." When Adel saw Itchale was not impressed by her wisdom, she embellished her plea with crying. "Please get rid of the gun." Adel rushed to Zelda to share with her the new development.

"And did he?" asked Zelda. "He refused."

"Oy vey to my life. All we need is a fighter!" cried Zelda.

"Don't worry. I begged and cried so hard that he had no choice but to return the gun."

"Men," said Zelda and sighed.

Itchale learned quickly not to underestimate his wife's determination to get whatever she set her mind on achieving.

"Mein tayere kind (my dear child)," said Zelda.

Adel gasped. She had never heard Zelda refer to her as "her child," let alone her "dear" child.

"Zelda, what is going on?"

"Ah, nothing," said Zelda, but her expression attested otherwise.

"Just foolish thoughts. People are saying there is going to be a horrible war. Worse than the previous one. I wish we could run away from here. But how can we run with the children? They are too young. And where to? You have at least Itchale's brother and sister in Russia. Look at those soldiers. They are getting ready to march across the river any day now. God only knows what plans they have for us." This tall, dark-haired, stoic woman, who always appeared to know it all, was scared and in tears.

Adel was shaking. The sisters, who knew how to comfort others, did not know how to console each other. They were not used to kind words nor a comforting hug. They stood next to each other mute in their worry and sorrow.

Zelda wiped her tears. "Adel, tayere." She repeated the "dear!"

*I must listen to her carefully*, Adel thought. *She is not herself.* "It's time for the two of you to escape to Russia," said Zelda, emphasizing her words. "You are young. Your whole life is ahead of you! Run my child! Save yourselves!"

Adel burst out crying. She turned to Zelda and embraced her. Zelda did not retreat. She submitted to the embrace with a deep sigh. The two sisters, one like a mother, the other like a child, cried in each other's arms. One final long overdue cry. A cry that echoed from the past and would continue into the days to come.

# 6
# Out of the Ditch

Adel and Itchale departed from their families with heavy hearts. And on a cold night in the early winter of 1940, they fled the shtetl. They joined three or four young couples, one of them with a child. From one of Adel's brothers, they borrowed a horse and carriage. One of the men in the group volunteered to be their coachman to take them to Lvov in Ukraine, Russia.

Lvov was approximately one hundred and fifty kilometers from Izbica, the closest Russian city on the border with Poland. As it turned out, their "coachman" was a shoemaker, who had never driven a horse and a carriage. Actually, he was scared of horses. However, staying in Izbica was even scarier. So he took the coachman's reins and, with a prayer, up they went.

On the night of their escape from the shtetl, the temperature dropped below zero. Adel and Itchale put on several layers of clothes. It kept them warm and there was less to carry. In a handbag, Adel packed a down blanket, a loaf of bread, a package of butter, a few apples, and a bottle of vodka to keep Itchale warm and happy. *After all, he had acquired some habits in the big city*, she thought. Usually, she did not approve of such habits like smoking and drinking. But these were unusual circumstances. Also, she wanted to show him she knew a few things about the world. She did not want to appear to her husband more provincial or ignorant than she really was. Above all, she wanted her husband's affection.

She was convinced that men—unlike women—need sex, a drink, and a smoke once in a while.

She noticed shortly after their wedding that when he came home from visiting with his friends, and a whiff of vodka was on his breath, he was particularly "friendly" to her. Not that she complained.

*Obviously, he does not need vodka to fuel his passion and love for me*, she thought, *not yet anyway.* She smiled at Itchale while letting him take a peek at what she had hidden in her handbag.

They brought a down blanket because it would keep them warm but mainly because they heard the Russians paid well for Polish down. If needed, they could sell it to buy food.

It was a moonless rainy night. The country roads were covered with ice. It appeared that neither the bespectacled coachman nor the horse saw very well. When they crossed over a creek, something scared the horse. It stood up on its hind legs, gave out a loud neigh, and turned over the carriage with its passengers straight into the icy water. Thank God, the rain had stopped and no one had drowned. The passengers crawled out one by one from underneath the overturned carriage and found their packages in the murky water.

However, the child who was on the carriage cried that he was hungry. His mother, instead of attending to him, was crying herself because she lost a small mirror, which fell out of her basket into the water. She had to find the mirror first.

*Look at that*, said Adel to herself. *She could have lost her child, but she is worried about her mirror. Go figure, people. You can never predict how a person behaves in an unexpected situation.*

Itchale was relieved to see Adel was not hurt. Not only that, she seemed to be in a good mood. Not panicky at all.

As if she is in overturned carriages every day. *What a character!* he thought.

While Itchale was helping others, Adel crawled out by herself. She did not ask for help nor expect to be helped.

To her surprise, she saw the coachman scratching his face and screaming, "Gotteniu in Himmel (God in Heaven). Help me! What have I done? I killed them!"

Adel burst out laughing. Needless to say, neither Itchale nor the coachman nor the passengers took it well. Itchale looked at her in disapproval.

Adel shrugged. She knew what life had taught her. Laughter is sometimes just another sound for crying.

Meanwhile, the horse released itself from the harness and galloped back home to Izbica.

The motion and commotion had called undesired attention. An angry peasant showed up on a horse, screaming and cursing. He was ready to call the local police officer. He calmed down only after one of the passengers offered him a "respectable" number of zloty if he promised to take them to Lvov instead of calling a policeman.

For that amount he said he was ready to take them even to Moscow.

He pulled the carriage from the creek, and with some "gentle" curses aimed mainly at "the mothers who brought these Jews into this world," he took them to Lvov.

When they arrived in the city, the passengers each went their own way. Adel and Itchale went looking for their family. They did not find Azriel at first, but they found Itchale's sister, Etel. This was the first time Adel had seen her sister-in-law. Etel was much older than Itchale and had lived in Lvov many years. Adel was impressed by this tall, dark-haired, gray-eyed woman. Her hair was fashionably short, combed to one side, revealing a long neck, adorned with a delicate golden necklace. Etel wore a simple but elegant dress with nice shoes. *She is definitely pretty*, thought Adel. I can see the resemblance between brother and sister.

The great joy of the meeting was marred by sadness and concern for both Itchale's and Adel's families left behind in Izbica.

Etel invited them to stay with her family in their three-bedroom apartment. The newlyweds spent a few days with Etel. There was a lot of catching up to do since the brother and sister had not seen each other in a long time. But although they were welcomed, it was crowded. And the young couple needed their privacy anyway. Itchale and Adel rented a tiny basement apartment in an affordable part of town and moved out.

A few days later, they went to the country to meet with Azriel and his family. The meeting was short because Azriel and his wife were already actively involved with Russian Jewish partisans. They were about to leave with their two young sons to join other partisans in the woods. Adel was afraid that Itchale, who was a bit of an idealist and an adventurer, might be tempted to get involved with that group as well.

She pleaded with him to go back to their apartment in Lvov. "I am a simple woman, Itchale. I never had any interests in political ideology. I just want to live peacefully, as much as possible, even in war times."

To her relief, Itchale promised her he would not join his brother.

Years after the war, Adel discovered that Azriel, his wife, and their two children were captured by the Nazis and executed by hanging. They were hanged separately. One tree for each.

In Lvov, they were refugees. Hungry and with no identification documents. In those years in Russia, a person without identification documents was considered a dead man if caught by the secret police, the NKVD. But documents or no documents, hunger conquers fear. They had no choice but to find work or sell some of the rags they had brought from Poland.

Itchale asked around for work but could not find any. However, there were rumors the Russian Communist government, which had taken over the Ukraine, was recruiting young men to work in the coal mines near the town of Donbass, over thirteen hundred kilometers from Lvov. The word in the street was every laborer would be paid about five hundred rubles a day—an enormous amount in those years. Many Jews signed up for that work. Itchale wanted to sign up, but Adel objected. She was afraid he would disappear, "God knows where." People disappeared without a trace in those days. "Besides, what do you know about coal mining?"

# 7
## "Menschlichkeit" — Compassion

When Adel resumed her search for Itchale, the world did not hold its breath. Itchale was her life, and she believed it was their destiny to be together.

Now, when he had suddenly disappeared, she would not stay at home and passively wait for him. Instead, she would take control over her life and go looking for him. She intended to go to the end of the world if needed and find him, alive or dead, God forbid.

No one noticed where and when, exactly, she began her journey. Probably, in the beginning of winter 1940, near a market square in Lviv, Ukraine.

At that time, Poland had been invaded by the Nazis. Jews were killed wherever captured or hunted. Others were sent to ghettos and from there to extermination camps. Izbica, Adel's and Izak's hometown, and the home of their families for generations—was not excluded. A few, like Adel and Itchale, escaped to Russia.

When Adel started walking, she was in her early twenties, a Polish Jewess who looked and spoke Polish like a gentile. A blonde beauty, with blue eyes and high cheekbones—genetic traces of her Swedish-Slavic ancestors. Because of her confident walk, she looked stronger and taller than she really was. She was a person of solid values and morals, courageous and determined but soft-hearted, humble and down to earth, and just like the mother she never knew, she was protective and devoted to those she loved. And she had loved her man for as long as she could remember.

Itchale, the love of her life, was in his twenties as well. A Polish Jew who unlike his wife looked more like his Mediterranean ancestors, a manly man. Generous and good-hearted but high-strung and hard working. Bright and well-read, who spoke fluently several languages; he had a quick humor and an acidic wittiness.

They were drawn to one another—feeling tied by intangible cords of the soul—pulled by destiny. She was determined to go forward and find Itchale; there was no looking back. At once, her life was divided into "before Itchale's disappearance" and "after." Adel started her walk, spellbound by love for her husband. Captivated by him but never submissive. She was free-spirited and proud of her courage to dare surviving on her own.

A new chapter in the story of her life began when she asked herself the pragmatic question, *How do I get from Lvov to Donbass in Eastern Ukraine?*

The peddler told her the distance between Lvov to the coal mines was about one thousand kilometers east. *How do I know which way is east? How will I find the coal mines?* she asked herself. Her Russian was poor at the time, and she could hardly read the Cyrillic characters.

*Foolish questions*, she thought. *I have to find him.*

Adel believed everything that happened from the moment she decided to find Itchale was meant to be.

Adel never made it to Donbass and the coal mines. She walked out of Lvov—looking like a Baba Yaga (a hag, a witch). She did not walk far when a Russian man with a horse and buggy stopped her. The man on the horse thought he recognized the young woman. But why was she wearing those clothes? Wasn't she the new Jewish refugee from Poland? he wondered. He was going to find out. It was his job to know.

"Devushka (young woman), Kto ty (who are you)? And where are you going?" His inquisitive tone did not leave any option of ignoring his question or pretending that she did not hear him. Adel knew she was at his mercy. She had no choice but to answer. In her limited Russian, she told him her husband had gotten a job in a coal mine near Donbass, and she was going to join him. To her surprise, instead of taking her to the police, he offered her a ride to the train station. When he noticed her hesitation, he assured Adel that he knew her husband.

"I know Izak. I respect a Jew who speaks our language and drinks our vodka like a true Russian," he said, smiling. "I know for a fact he was not sent to the coal mines. He was put on a truck that went elsewhere. Maybe to the Ural Mountains, to Siberia, or even to Mongolia."

"How do you know that? Did you see him?" Adel dared to ask.

"I know," he said. "And you don't need to know how I know."

It was safer to avoid raising his suspicion by asking more questions. With some hesitation, she climbed into the buggy.

"My husband is waiting for me. He probably told you we are newlyweds. So you understand that I have to be with him.

Mne nuzhna pomashch (I need help). How do I get to the Ural? To Siberia or Mongolia?"

For an unknown reason, the Russian man was moved by this young woman. Even the rags she wore did not make her ugly. "Izak, what a lucky bastard," he muttered under his mustache. "Don't worry," he said in a softer voice. "You will find your husband. Go east, and ask your people." He meant other Jews. "They are everywhere. With some luck, you'll find him. And now, enough talking. I will take you to the train station."

Adel was speechless. A million thoughts raced in her mind at once. *Is it really happening? Who is he? Can I trust him? I have to get to the station. Whatever is meant to be—will be,* she reassured herself.

Only when she got off his buggy and sat safely in the train did she think about the stranger's behavior. Was it a miracle? She was not sure. Miracles were recognized as such only after the fact anyway. In any event, it was an act of "menschlichkeit" (humaneness, compassion)—found even when she least expected it.

# 8

# A Dark-Haired Man with Burning Eyes

The first day of Adel's journey started with a miracle or with an act of menschlichkeit by a stranger on a horse. The following was about to be blessed with another miracle.

The Russian man who had brought her to the train station told her the Ural Mountains were about two thousand kilometers from Lvov. "Much closer than Siberia or Mongolia."

*Great comfort*, she thought.

She did not know if the little money she had was enough for a ticket to the closer destination—the Ural Mountains. Actually, it was enough only for the first stop of the train.

Not long after she got on the train, the rattling rhythm cradled her to sleep. For a few hours, she was rid of the anxiety of that morning and the uncertainty of the future. That was probably the sweetest sleep she had had in a long time.

Several hours later, a conductor ordered her off the train.

She found herself in a rural area, near a small village. A dirt road lined by an orchard led to the village. Adel did not know where she was. But it made no difference, as long as she was going in the right direction to the Ural Mountains. She was not going to stay in the village long enough to remember its name anyway.

It was getting dark and colder. She was tired and hungry and knew she had to find a place to sleep. In her basket, she still had the butter and a few slices of the bread she had brought with her from Lvov. That would take care of her hunger. What was she to do next?

Adel noticed a woman villager, carrying two heavy baskets, who got off the train. She walked over to the woman and asked if she needed help in carrying her baskets. Although the woman did not seem to be alarmed by the vagabond, she nevertheless rejected the offer.

When Adel realized the woman did not walk away from her, she ventured to ask her if there was a place in the village to stay for the night. Adel had nothing to lose. She could not be deterred by meager rejection. *I am desperate*, she thought.

The woman nodded and gestured to Adel to follow her. As they came closer to the village, a mixed breed dog greeted them. The dog wiggled its tail and barked indiscriminately at the stranger and its owner alike. From a cottage came running a couple of young children, a boy and a girl. As they noticed the stranger, they stopped running, stuck their thumbs in their mouths, and stared at her the way only children can stare.

*I must look like an old witch*, she thought. *I am surprised they do not run away screaming.*

The woman invited Adel into her home. It was a humble cottage with a thatched roof, similar to Adel's home in Izbica. Near the entrance door were a small vegetable garden, a well, and a kennel for the dog. She could also smell some farm animals, but they were not in sight. The air was crisp and cold and full of calm noises of families gathering at the end of the day for an evening meal. *As if there was no war in the world*, she thought. *As if life could be normal.*

A log was burning in a brick stove. Around a heavy wooden table were seated her husband, a stocky-looking man with a big mustache, and the two children she saw earlier. They looked like twins, still sucking their thumbs. They were staring at her shyly. The dog was howling in the yard, calling attention to itself. Adel asked where she could wash her face and her hands. The woman pointed to the yard. After Adel was refreshed, she came in and sat at the table.

She then introduced herself. "My name is Adel." The husband smiled and repeated, "Adela." She did not correct him. "Adela" sounded more mature and ladylike. *Vain thoughts*, she thought.

The husband pointed at himself and said their names in order of importance. His name first, then his wife's, his children's, and last, their dog's. They all laughed, even the kids. The ice was broken. The dog, Boris, was a member of the family. Adel remembered only Lena, the woman's name, and the dog's. Maybe because she had heard those before. The others were foreign to her. The husband and wife spoke Ukrainian between themselves and in Russian to Adel.

They did not waste more time on chatting and started eating. Lena put on the table a good meal—a freshly baked loaf of bread, a chunk of unidentified meat, a few potatoes, and a jar of milk. Gratefully, Adel ate a slice of bread, one potato, and drank a cup of milk. She did not touch the meat. Not because it was not "kosher"—she believed that survival takes priority over religious commandments—but because she was fastidious. Regardless of how starved she ever was, she would not put in her mouth anything that she did not know the origin of or was regarded as unclean.

As they started eating, Adel pulled out the package of butter which she had brought with her and put it on the table.

*I do not have money to pay them for their hospitality*, she thought, *so that is my gift.*

Both husband and wife thanked her several times. The woman took a tiny spoonful of the butter and tasted it. She nodded in approval. The butter was good. Adel was pleased. Now that her hunger was fed, she felt sleepy. Lena noticed and led her outside to a hut attached to the cottage. She put a blanket on the floor, spread some hay on it, and threw another blanket on top. That was to be Adel's bed for the night. It was dark, so she could not tell if she was alone in the hut. But by the smell, she could tell the family's goat had been kicked out of its bedroom. She thought, *I hope that it's not a vindictive goat waiting for me in the morning.* That was her last thought before she fell asleep, smiling.

Adel fell asleep so fast that when the morning light woke her up, she was sure she had not slept at all. Was she ready to greet the day? No! She had hoped that Itchale's disappearance was just another bad dream. And she would wake up at home, wherever home was, as long as he was with her.

When Adel got up, Lena, her husband, and their kids were all gone to their daily chores. At the side of her bed, Adel found a loaf of fresh bread, a cup of milk, and half the package of butter, which Lena had left for her. Adel drank the milk, put the bread in her basket, and left the butter for the family.

Adel waved goodbye to Boris, took a deep breath, and walked back to the railroad tracks. She did not know where else to go, except to continue toward the Ural.

*How far am I from the mountains?* she wondered. *And when I arrive in the mountains—what then?* She told herself, "One thing at a time."

A train passed by the village. It did not stop. The railroad tracks stretched beyond the horizon. Adel was probably about five hundred kilometers from where she had started her search. If she took the train all the way to the Ural Mountains, she would have had another two thousand kilometers ahead.

Even if she could have afforded the train, would she find her husband there?

How, in chaotic times, does a woman start a search for her man? She had a simple answer. "Adel, you put one foot in front of the other and start walking. You go to where your heart leads you, and you ask, 'Have you seen a dark-haired man with burning eyes?'"

# 9
# Mountains on the Horizon

Adel faced the railroad tracks stretching from horizon to horizon. From east to north. She had no knowledge of distances or the geography of the country. Feathery snowflakes swirled in the cold air. No dog was barking, no bird chirping, and no train was huffing. The squeak of her steps in the snow was the only sound that tore the silence. Her stride was light and steady still. The snow was not deep yet, and the ground underneath was frozen. After her stay in the Ukraine village, she was well rested and not hungry. The loaf of bread lay like a promise in her basket.

She walked ten or twelve kilometers until her feet could not carry her further. She sat down on the tracks, pulled out the bread, and took a bite. She almost broke her teeth. The bread was frozen. To quiet the pangs of hunger, she put a handful of snow into her mouth. This was how she silenced her hunger for a while. Adel looked around. There was no village in sight. Not a house, not a person, not an animal. Only trees and shrubs and the railroad tracks lost in the bleached horizon.

*I have to leave the tracks and look for a village*, she thought. *There, I may find something to eat, a ride to continue my journey, or a place to stay. Which direction should I go?* she asked herself. *Always forward*, she promised herself. *To where my heart leads me.*

And her heart carried her further in spite of her fatigue and hunger. She kept walking until she heard dogs barking. Barking meant people were not too far. "I have always been afraid of dogs. But it is time to overcome that fear," she said aloud.

The barking led her into a village. A thick blanket of snow covered everything in sight. It did not take long before a man came out to check on the commotion.

"Kto ty (who are you)?" he asked.

"I am Adel," she answered quickly. *He speaks Russian not Ukrainian*, she thought. *Good. How much closer am I to the Ural Mountains? To Siberia?*

"I am on my way to the Ural to join my husband. I need a place to stay, and I am willing to work for it."

The man measured her up from top to bottom. With a stern glance, he pondered the information he gathered by looking at her and listening to her answer. She knew he was trying to read between the lines of what was not said, and he could not make up his mind. Should he invite her in or should he get rid of her?

*How long will it take him to decide what to do?* she thought.

She was shivering, not only because of the cold wind but also because she felt as if she was standing in front of a judge, waiting for his verdict.

The arctic wind and Adel's pitiful appearance urged him to make a decision.

He pointed to a small shed. "You can stay there for the night. We'll talk in the morning."

She blessed him in the names of the Holy Mother and her Son. *He might be an atheist*, she thought. *But I am quite sure he will not reject a blessing from a Baba Yaga.*

It was safer to appear as a Polish Baba Yaga on any given day, but especially in those days, than a proud Jewess.

Survival, she believed, sometimes dictates the need to bend down pride or rules.

She stepped into the dark shed and was welcomed by a myriad of overwhelming odors of whatever the villager stored in that shed. The darkness was impenetrable and scary. She was afraid to step on a sleepy snake (they sleep in the wintertime; that much she knew) or on a person. In the pitch darkness of the shed, both were equally frightening. However, she let out a sudden cry when she realized she had stumbled on a dog, not on a person or a snake. The dog was too sleepy or too lazy to bark. Her body froze in place. *Is it going to bite me?*

The dog acknowledged her presence by opening one eye. It went right back to sleep. She was of no threat nor interest. She sighed in relief. *This sleepy guardian, too, will have a talk with me in the morning.*

Growing up in a shtetl, Adel knew dogs represented danger. At times, gentiles used to unleash dog attacks on Jews. However, on that night, the presence of a dog—a living being which did not try to harm her—was consoling. She lay down a safe distance from the dog. The whistle of the blowing wind penetrated the cracks in the shed's walls, sending shivers throughout her body. The arctic wind was an alarming reminder of what was awaiting her in the days to come. She curled up in the blanket the man left for her on the floor, pressing her basket—her entire possessions on earth—to her chest. The night was long and cold. Her teeth were chattering so loud she was afraid it might wake up the dog. Her sense of humor, as in normal times, was intact.

Adel's thoughts raced. *Is this how my life is going to be from now on? Did I make the right decision? When will it end? Ah, foolish thoughts. I am looking for Itchale. That's it. I cannot afford feeling sorry for myself or be afraid of any passing shadow. This is my life now. One day at a time.* She finally dozed off at dawn with a comforting thought. The villager's welcome was a good omen.

With daylight, the peasant and his wife stepped into the shed. They seemed to be surprised to find her alive. Adel blessed them again when they invited her into their cottage. They introduced themselves as "Natalia" and "Alexey." Natalia handed her a towel and a bowl with warm water to wash herself. Afterward, Natalia gave her a cup of hot tea and a thick slice of bread with butter.

*Like the couple in Ukraine,* she thought, *they were true life-savers, and they didn't even know it.*

In poor Russian, but in fluent body language, Adel told them she was from Poland, a newlywed on her way to join her husband who found work in the coal mines in the Ural area. It was not safe to tell them he disappeared or anything else closer to the truth. Adel explained she had spent her money on the trip thus far and, therefore, needed to work and a place to stay until she could continue her travel. Natalia shrugged and looked at her husband. The exchange of looks between husband and wife told Adel they had understood there was more to her story, but it was better not to ask. In the atmosphere of suspicion and fear of those days, a host of a spouse of a probable "enemy of the people" could have easily been considered an enemy himself.

Adel did not miss the exchange of looks. *But why did they take the risk of inviting me into their home?* she wondered.

Natalia was good but tough. Alexey had the soft heart. He was not the stern judge he had appeared to be the night before when Adel showed up on their doorstep. He told her she could stay for as long as she needed.

"You are good people," she told them.

Adel was grateful for their charitable behavior, but she was also remorseful for what she felt the day before. *I stood in fear in front of the kindest man and felt judged by him when he was thinking how to help me. It was my fear of being judged. It had little to do with him. I felt small and worthless, just the way I felt many times during my childhood. Will I know, next time, the difference between cautiousness and mistrust? Careful questioning and judging? Will I ever stop being afraid? I am a grown woman now, not a helpless child.*

Natalia, encouraged by her husband's response, asked her what kind of work she was capable of doing. Adel listed all she thought she could do to help Natalia—clean the house, cook well, take care of their children, and help with their farm animals. She was ready to do any work needed. Natalia liked Adel's answer. Adel cleaned Natalia's house and other houses in the village. She cooked, learned to milk goats and cows, fed the dogs, and bathed babies. And in the process, she improved her Russian. She had to learn fast if she wanted to befriend the villagers and get as many paid jobs as she could take. Natalia taught her the Cyrillic alphabet, so she could read Russian.

Russia, Poland, Germany—the world was at war, but the battlefront was far. The war had little impact yet on the village life. A few families sent their husbands or sons to the army, but there were no casualties to mourn yet. No one went hungry.

Adel consoled herself that being a Polish citizen and an illegal refugee in Russia, Itchale could not serve in the army.

She worked hard, but she enjoyed her physical strength, and it took her mind off her foolish thoughts. Best of all, she was pleased she could earn her stay and save some to continue her journey. During the daytime, she kept herself busy. The villagers loved to hear her singing Polish and Russian songs. Her laughter echoed in the village's alleys and made people smile.

"You look like one of us. How come? You are Polish," they said. With her blonde hair and Slavic cheekbones, she did. It amused her. *And as a Polish girl did they expect me to have horns?* she thought.

But at nightfall, the happy, easygoing mask of daytime came off. Darkness took over. Her mind stirred up frightening images of what might have happened to Itchale. *What will happen to me if, God forbid, I find out he is gone forever? What happened with our families? Will I ever see them again? How will I live if anything happened to those I love?*

She would usually cry herself to sleep. Only the dog witnessed her silent crying. And his indifference was comforting. Adel did not want any attention. She was used to taking care of herself and took pride in it.

Because she knew the depth of darkness at night, she enjoyed the brightness of the day with no guilt or remorse.

Time flew by quickly. The winter was almost over. The snow started to melt, and it was not as cold. New buds peeked out shyly from tree branches. Spring was in the air. Adel knew that it was time to say goodbye to Natalia and Alexey and continue her search for Itchale.

Natalia and Alexey walked her to the train station. She liked them, and they had treated her like one of their own. By the time the train arrived, they were all in tears. They kissed her on her cheeks and were still waving goodbye even after the train was moving.

# 10
# Itchale — The Missing Part

"One-way ticket please to the Ural." Adel hoped she would not need a return ticket.

"You can get off in Sverdlovsk (Yekaterinburg)," said the woman at the ticket counter.

"How far is it from here?" asked Adel.

"It is more than two thousand five hundred kilometers away. You will have plenty of time to rest," she said with a smile.

*Sverdlovsk sounds familiar*, thought Adel. She recalled from her history book that it was a historical city, the city where Tsar Nicholas and the Romanov family were killed by the Bolsheviks during the October Revolution. She shook her head. *The foolish thoughts that pop into my head! Is Itchale there? Where should I look for him?*

Adel was not too worried. She had some money to buy food. She was wearing better boots and a warm man's jacket, which Alexey gave her, and it was getting warmer.

The train was crowded and dirty with the foul smells of people confined in a small space for days and nights. Sweat, urine, and unfamiliar food, all were nauseating. As always, Adel found the silver lining even in that miserable situation. *I am glad I found a seat at a window, although it is hard and broken. I will probably feel every bone in my body at the end of that journey, but at least I am on the train to the Ural.*

The commotion of a couple of drunkards in the cabin kept her alert. *You never know what those drunk men are capable of,* she thought.

She was glued to the sights outside. The filthy window caused the rapidly moving views to look as if shrouded in fog. She watched the landscape with a glazed stare. After a while, she lost track of time. The train crossed over bridges and rivers, lakes and creeks. Where the snow had melted, she could see patches of green fields and orchards adorned with pink and white blooming buds like dresses on the trees. She fantasized about being back one day for a train ride, but as a free person, not a haunted one, and with Itchale. Together they would enjoy this abundance of beauty.

The days got longer and the nights shorter. She did not engage in idle conversations nor was she curious about the other passengers. In fact, most passengers, just like her, kept to their own business. It was not a joyous ride for anybody. Russia was at war, and millions of people were relocated voluntarily or involuntarily. Attention giving or attention drawing was not appreciated.

War or not, nature celebrated itself with no concern or care for anybody's condition—Adel's included. Nature's awakening forced her to be aware of her youthful vitality and femininity. And it recharged her with energy to find her man.

After days and nights of rattling and jingling, shaking, huffing, and honking, the train was slowing down, getting ready to rest. "The next stop—Sverdlovsk!" announced the conductor.

Swiping the fogged-up window with the palm of her hand, she made an arch to look through at the approaching vista.

*Could the roundish-looking mountains on the horizon be the Ural Mountains? Finally?* She was anxious, anticipating the future, while excited at the same time.

As the train pulled closer to the station, the city revealed itself in an elegant turret of a church and in old buildings retaining the beauty of a kinder era.

Nauseated by the shaking and rattling of the train and after days in the crowded train cabin, Adel could hardly wait to get off. She sat on a bench at the station. It felt good to breathe fresh air, to be on solid ground again, and to simply take a moment for herself.

Watching people of all races, listening to languages she had never heard before, and strolling the nicely paved boulevards lined with their straight, disciplined old trees, she relaxed. She liked the old, ornamented buildings in fading soft colors from a friendlier time. They seemed to be overlooking in pity, the new, tall, and severe-looking buildings that were identical in style—like soldiers wearing gray uniforms.

Adel enjoyed watching the big cathedrals and white churches with their golden onion-like domes. She admired the colorful gardens and the larger-than-life statues of heroic figures from Russian history.

*I have to pinch myself. I am in a big city, in the Ural Mountains region.*

*Enough strolling,* she thought. *I have to find a marketplace and perhaps an office for Jewish affairs.*

She also had to find a place to stay for the night and something to eat.

During the long train ride, with the little cash she had, she had bought a loaf of bread and a package of butter. That was all she could afford.

Bread, not butter, had special meaning to Adel. She used to say, "As long as I have bread, I feel safe. All I want is a slice of bread, fresh or stale. I am not greedy. I don't ask for a whole loaf of bread, just a slice or even a bite."

She took off her head kerchief and let her hair fall free on her shoulders. "Ah, it feels so good to take that 'shmatte' (rag) off my head," she said aloud.

For a few moments, she was a young woman, free to dare the day with her sunny hair.

In a park, surrounded by flowers, she was in a contemplative mood. *I am only a simple woman*, she thought. *What do I need to make me happy? A slice of bread, a blooming flower, a kind word, laughter, and my loved ones. Although some money would not hurt either.*

*So why do tears roll down my cheeks? Because I am a silly woman. I cry when it cries itself. And I laugh when it laughs itself.*

Adel knew from experience how fragile life was. Loss and grief were part of her life since birth. And since grief was a constant companion, she would allow herself to occasionally take a break from grief and enjoy the moment, without feeling as if she had betrayed anyone—alive or deceased.

The simplicity of beauty around her juxtaposed the complexity of her situation. She was acutely aware of the missing part in her life—Itchale.

She wiped her tears, put her head kerchief on, and got up. She had to explore the city further, gather information, and ask what needed to be asked to find her man.

Adel crossed a bridge over the mighty Iset River. A sign on the riverbank read: "The Iset flows over six hundred kilometers from the Urals through Sverdlovsk into the Tobol River." She was pleased to be able to read the Russian Cyrillic letters.

Across the river, on the horizon, almost at hand-reaching distance, she saw the Ural Mountains. The majestic view caused her heart to contract in pain. Itchale, Itchale, Itchale. She tried to will him over with her thoughts, with the calling of her heart. If she could only cross the river and fly over the mountains and find his hiding place—

While walking back to the city, she noticed out of the corner of her eye someone watching her intently. He was not a police officer, just an older man who looked like a refugee. *Who was he? He looked familiar. Where have I seen this face?* she wondered.

She felt uncomfortable but not scared. *I'd better confront him first rather than wait to be confronted*, she thought.

So, with some trepidation, she walked over to the man and asked him in Russian, "Why are you watching me? Do you know me?"

To her relief, he responded in Yiddish. "I noticed you at the train station. You seemed to be lost a bit. I thought that like me, you came from Poland. I am looking for relatives from my town. Where are you from?"

Adel did not let her guard down. *He might be an NKVD informer who speaks Yiddish*, she thought.

There were rumors about informants like that. She answered in a question. "Where are you from?"

"From Lublin," he answered. "I live here now."

Izbica was close enough to Lublin. *He might be harmless after all,* she thought. *What a foolish thought. What does the distance of Izbica from Lublin have to do with that man's potential dangerousness?*

However, she needed help, so she ignored her suspicion. "I am from a shtetl near Lublin, and I am looking for my husband. He was sent to work in this area. Is there a 'gulag' (a forced labor camp) here?"

She could tell the man was capable of completing what she omitted. He did not know of any gulags in the area. But he knew where the marketplace was. "This is a good place to meet people and ask around. But be cautious who you ask and what," he advised her.

These last words were enough to remove the last shadow of suspicion Adel had toward the man. She noticed, however, they never introduced themselves to each other by name through their entire conversation.

*Why do I look suspicious to him?* she wondered but thanked him anyway.

"You came to the right place," he told her. "Sverdlovsk is the administrative city of the Ural region. So you may find somebody here with helpful information. But for your own sake, I hope that you don't develop high hopes. Trying to find your husband here would probably be as easy as looking for a needle in a haystack."

Those words hit her in the gut. She was ready to walk away when he asked, "What's your husband's name? What does he look like?"

"Izak. Itchale. He is twenty-two years old, about your height. He is dark-haired with green burning eyes."

"Burning eyes?"

"If you saw him, you'd understand." She smiled, slightly embarrassed. "You cannot forget his eyes."

He had not seen her Itchale.

*Poor woman*, he thought. *Love blinds her. "Burning eyes"—whoever heard of such a thing?*

Adel felt as if the earth had swallowed Itchale. She was going to throw up. *Pull yourself together, Adel*, she commanded herself. *Take a deep breath and lift your head.*

The man did not notice her turmoil or perhaps he pretended not to notice. He did not want to get further involved.

However, the man was helpful about food. He pointed to a street nearby. "There's a soup kitchen for refugees set up by Jewish people. It is not far from here. I was there myself. Nothing to be ashamed of," he added gently.

"I am too hungry to be ashamed," she replied, rejecting his gentleness. He understood the underlying message: Don't get closer. They parted quickly.

# 11
# "Masha, Have Mercy"

The long line of people waiting and yelling, "Masha, Masha, have mercy," was a clue she had arrived at the right place—the soup kitchen.

Masha, the woman in charge of distributing the soup, was not impressed by the yelling. Days of standing on her feet, watching hungry people uprooted from their homes, and inhaling the vapors of the foul soup she had to serve had hardened her heart. She had her own story. She did not look like one of the misfortunate people she served, but she was one of them. However, she was among the lucky ones, one who had a job and could get more than a slice of bread a day.

Adel joined the line and waited and waited a bit longer. By the time it was her turn to receive the watery liquid and the slice of bread, she was about to faint. She took the bowl of soup with shaking hands and dunked a half slice of bread to give it some substance. She put the second half in her basket, for tomorrow. While sipping the soup, as slowly as she could, she watched Masha at work. Despite her dark hair and a hint of a mustache, she had surprisingly soft eyes. Adel wondered if Masha was Jewish? Would it make a difference?

*If I have to stay in this city until I find Itchale, I'd better find work. Let's see if this woman can help me,* she thought.

Adel waited until Masha took a break. She then introduced herself to Masha in Yiddish, the international language of Jewish refugees from Eastern Europe. "What do you want?" replied the woman rudely.

"I am looking for my husband. You see many people every day. Perhaps you have seen him?"

Adel repeated the description of the dark-haired man with burning eyes, twenty-two years old, who was sent to a gulag in the Urals.

"No. It does not sound familiar," said Masha.

Adel did not give up. "Where else is it safe to ask about him? How far are the gulags?"

Masha looked at her with both annoyance and pity and said in Yiddish, "You are young, and even with the rags you are wearing, I can tell that you are pretty enough to find another man. Forget him. If he was sent to a gulag—he will never see the daylight again. No one leaves those camps. And you don't want to be thrown into jail because you've asked too many questions." Masha almost whispered the last words.

Adel felt dizzy. Masha rushed to catch her before she fell. Someone rushed with a cup of water. The color came back to her face. She rubbed her temples with her fingers. *What should I do now?* For some reason, her heart was telling her Masha was wrong.

*I feel Itchale is alive!* Her heart was pounding. *Is this wishful thinking?* She kept those feelings to herself.

Adel told Masha that since her situation was dire, she should stay in the city, find work and a place to live. She was not going to share her plans of continuing to look for her husband with anybody.

*I can rely only on myself. And trust only what comes out of my mouth.*

Masha was intrigued by the young woman who appeared from nowhere and was looking for her husband. *Is she naïve? Is she insane, God forbid? Or is there something else that brought her here?* Masha wondered.

Whatever the reason, Masha needed help in the soup kitchen and with her ailing mother at home. The young woman seemed gentle and good-mannered. *Better to keep her here*, she thought. Masha gestured to Adel to step aside and wait for her.

Adel was not going to wait idly until Masha finished her shift. While Masha was distributing the soup, Adel walked into the kitchen and started cleaning dishes, thinking that no one was paying attention.

Adel did not notice, but Masha did pay attention. And she liked what she saw.

"Adel," she said, "you got yourself a job. I cannot pay you, but you will not go hungry. We work in the kitchen in shifts. If you wish, you can stay in my place. I live with my mother in a small apartment, but I can make room for you. I will not charge you rent if you are willing to also take care of my mother and clean our apartment."

Adel could not believe her good fortune. In a matter of minutes, she went from devastation to elation.

*This is another good omen*, she thought. She almost kissed Masha in gratitude. Except one look at her mustache and Adel withdrew.

Adel stayed in Sverdlovsk a few months until she gathered more information about forced labor camps, possible routes to get around, and about the whereabouts of men sent to gulags. Without telling a soul, she walked the streets of the city day by day, always looking for Itchale.

Wandering the streets paid off. One day, she heard that Polish Jews were sent to gulags in Novosibirsk, the capital of Siberia. They said there were no labor camps near Sverdlovsk, but rather "somewhere between Sverdlovsk and Novosibirsk, about sixteen hundred kilometers east."

Now, she had a new direction for her search. She had to get ready to continue forward. Because of her work at the kitchen, she did not go hungry; however, it did not pay in cash. Masha, on the other hand, paid her for attending her mother and their apartment. Adel saved those rubles. She was healthy and eager to continue her journey.

One evening, at the end of her shift in the kitchen, Adel packed a basket with bread, butter, and a small jar of marmalade. Once in a blue moon, she felt rich when she could afford to buy something sweet.

*My life is bitter enough. Don't I deserve to sweeten it a little?* she said to herself.

The next morning, when the sun barely peeked over the horizon, Adel put on her Baba Yaga attire. Masha was awake already. She stood straight like a guard by the door with a stern expression.

"I have something in my eye," she mumbled, avoiding Adel's eyes. The two women shook hands and exchanged a few formal blessings. Adel kissed the teary mother and walked out with a light step but with heaviness in her chest.

Once again, she had separated from people she was attached to. Attachment, she believed, was like an addiction. You can indulge in it or decide to quit cold turkey.

She quit. To continue her journey to the unknown. Perhaps to another attachment.

# 12
## Standing in Line

It was fall already, and Adel was heading farther east to Novosibirsk.

She walked for days and lost their count. One day was like the next and the one before. At daylight, she walked and at nightfall, she found a clearing in a field or an abandoned shed near a village to spend the night. She was not welcomed in any of the villages she walked by. Peasants unleashed dogs on her or even hit her when she got too close. She ate whatever wild fruit she could find on trees and in the fields, but she was still hungry. Hunger weakened her body and clouded her mind. All she could think of was a slice of bread, even a bite would do.

The days were getting shorter and the cold nights longer. Winter was approaching faster than she had expected.

*I have to find a place to stay through the winter*, she thought.

It was a cold but sunny day. Suddenly, her feet had a will of their own. Her body felt like a balloon emptied from air in one whish. She had no will power left to move forward. It was the first time Itchale was not on her mind. She fell to the ground without feeling the fall. She opened her eyes and saw smoking chimneys on the horizon.

Something like a jolt of lightning went through her body. *Itchale, here I come!*

She jumped to her feet in a surge of energy she did not believe she still had in her. She forgot her hunger and her achy feet. She almost ran toward the smoking chimneys. She stopped at a sign on a small, unassuming gate that read "Asbestos factory in the municipality of Asbest." That was the name of the town. Adel looked around. There was no one at the gate. But at some distance not too far from the gate, she saw people standing in a long and silent line. They did not wear uniforms. That was a good sign. Perhaps it was not a prison. But it did not look like a labor camp either.

*Hunger beats fear*, she thought.

Now, she had another opportunity to prove it to herself. She walked through the gate and, with little hesitation, joined the line, as if she had done it for days.

Those who stood in line did not seem to pay attention to her. Some of them might have been newcomers like her.

*They may be waiting for a meal*, she thought. *As long as no one kicks me out of the line, I have nothing to lose.*

It turned out she had joined workers of an asbestos factory, waiting for their first meal of the day. Each person was handed a tin cup and a bowl, and some liquid was poured into both. A chunk of dark bread was added to the bowl. The woman who distributed the meal asked her for a food card. Adel did not expect that.

"I lost it," she said looking straight in the woman's eyes.

The woman gave her a quick look and, without a word, handed her the meal, as if she had been seeing her every day. Adel took the meal and, with her head down, avoided making any unwanted eye contact. She found a far corner in the yard and sat down to eat. The "lunch break" was over shortly, and people lined up again to return their dishes. Adel did the same. A new line was formed. Adel joined that one too. Without a look or a word, she was handed an apron, gloves, and a head kerchief and was sent to one of the buildings. Mostly women were standing on both sides of long and narrow tables. Adel watched what the other women did and did the same. She learned that day the factory manufactured products for the Soviet air force.

*Am I lucky or what?* she thought. She felt like dancing. She had a paying job! *Itchale, will I have stories to tell you! You just wait!*

A few hours later and she had already befriended a couple of women. They noticed her from the moment she joined the food line at noon, they told her, but they did not turn her in. They did not need to hear her story to understand her situation. They advised her to tell the table's supervisor she had been ill and, therefore, did not come to work and she had lost the food card that enabled her to get two meals a day.

At the end of the day, each laborer received half a loaf of bread, a cup of tea, and a bowl of some warm liquid, namely soup. They worked twelve hours a day and were paid less than two rubles an hour. Single women, like Adel, stayed in separate quarters. About forty women slept in one long hall that looked like an overground bunker. Two rows of iron beds were lined up along the concrete walls. Each had a grass mattress covered by a gray sheet and a brown woolen blanket. A few lucky ones managed to get pillows. There was one door and no windows. Two light bulbs were on day and night. The air inside was always stuffy and sickening. As expected, some women were friendlier or more curious than others. Adel made friends but kept her distance. She never let her guard down entirely. Nobody suspected she was Jewish. The women liked her and were protective of her, especially the older ones. She was not afraid of hard labor; she never complained and was always ready to help. They loved to hear her singing in Polish, Ukrainian, and Russian. And they thought her laughter was contagious. Even if one of the women heard her crying late at night, nobody asked her about it. Each one had reasons to laugh in the daytime and to cry at night.

Adel was cautious but persistent about her inquiries into a gulag in that area. Her closest friends advised her not to ask "those questions." Nobody had heard of any gulag or so she was told. She kept gathering information, never sharing her plans with anyone. Her cover story was she had been born in Poland but lived in Lvov and she was looking for her husband who went to the Urals to find work. Whether her friends believed her or not did not matter as long as they did not tell on her. Adel kept working there until she saved enough money to continue her journey.

It was springtime already. One morning, a minute after the siren announced it was time to get up for work, she did not get up from bed, pretending to be ill. She did not show up to work. Instead, she got dressed, took her basket, and walked out without anyone's notice.

Had she been caught—a deserter from a governmental factory, from the war effort of Mother Russia?—Unheard of!—she would have ended up in jail or worse.

She was ready to risk it all. *My life is not worth anything without Itchale*, she thought.

"Davai (come on), Adel!" she ordered herself in Russian. "Put one foot in front of the other, and go! Davai!"

# CROSSING THE CONTINENTS TO THE EAST

# 13
## A Smiling Basket

No one heard her when she commanded herself to go. "Davai!"

No one noticed when she put one foot in front of the other and started walking toward Novosibirsk. She was just a passing shadow in a world of turmoil.

It was raining, and she was crying. Her tears salted the raindrops running off her cheeks. Were those tears of loneliness? Of self-pity? Or of longing for Itchale?

*No time for crying, Adel*, she thought. She collected herself. *Keep walking. What a relief. I am drenched in tears and rain, but at least I am not thirsty.* She shrugged.

Now it was spring. The snow had melted, and the days were getting warmer. Adel started walking early in the morning, and by midday, she was tired and hungry. Blackberry bushes that grew on the edges of the railroad tracks looked like the berries she used to pick in Poland. Without hesitation, she plucked a handful and put them in her mouth.

"Oh my god!" she exclaimed. "These berries are as sour and bitter as my life!" She spat them out in disgust.

*Have You Seen a Dark-Haired Man with Burning Eyes?* 75

She scooped up a fistful of water from a nearby creek and drank until the bitterness in her mouth was washed away. She felt a surge of energy. The drink of clear water lifted her spirit, and she was ready to go on.

There was no village in sight, no person, only some bushy-tailed foxes running across the tracks. *As long as they are running far from me, I'm fine*, she shuddered. It was getting dark. Adel had to find a place to stay for the night. She was afraid it was going to be another night in the wilderness.

Fear joined hunger as her loyal companions. When fear became overwhelming, she would feel numbness—detachment from everything around her. In those moments, she did not feel aches and pain and hunger. She was present in body only. Her spirit was somewhere else.

*There is only so much that my heart can take*, she said to herself.

But to stay numb was a luxury she could not afford for too long. She had to keep going.

She got busy doing what needed to be done to survive the night. That evening, like so many evenings before when she had to sleep in the wilderness, she looked for a clearing behind trees or bushes in order to not be seen by a passing train. She made sure there were no holes in the ground because of her fear of crawling creatures or four-legged ones who might be hiding in those dark holes. Even if she had matches, she could not make a fire—it was too dangerous. A fire could be seen from a distance and draw unwanted attention. But above all, she tried to hold back any frightening thoughts that something horrible might have happened to Itchale.

The last rays of sun lured her to relax, to take a deep breath, and to enjoy nature.

*I have never noticed there is a moment of silence between sunset and nightfall,* she thought in wonderment. *As if God holds his breath when light battles darkness.*

The world went silent. Birds and crickets did not chirp and wolves did not howl. There was not the slightest wind to move the leaves on the trees.

And then, all at once, with the fall of darkness, the whole world came alive again. The hustle and bustle of busy birds looking for a place to build a nest for the night; crickets practicing their singing, trying to avoid becoming a bedtime snack for hungry beaks.

"How could I be so blind?" she asked loudly. "I have been walking in the Siberian taiga forest for days now and never paid close attention to its beauty."

*Beauty is like a double-edged sword,* she thought. *It's tempting and enticing to lose yourself in it. But losing yourself can be dangerous.*

And the taiga was dangerous. It was deceptive in its beauty. Bears, wolves, and other animals roamed the woods. Snakes crawled in the tall grass. Biting insects hid in colorful wildflowers, and poisonous berries grew, perfectly camouflaged, on inviting bushes.

She lay down with a deep sigh, her basket under her head as a pillow. The chirping and howling, her fears and fatigue took their toll, and she finally fell asleep. She was half-frozen when the first daylight woke her up. She realized two things: first, she had survived another night in the wilderness and, second, it was not raining.

*Both are good signs*, she thought.

She decided to follow the railroad tracks of the Trans-Siberian train so she would not get lost. She was surrounded by the dense forests of the taiga. Pine, birch, spruce, and larch trees in all shades of green; hills and creeks of bubbling water. But walking too close to the tracks was dangerous—she would risk being seen by passengers of passing trains.

*What isn't dangerous?* she asked herself. *Walking in the forest or through a village is not dangerous? I have to take a risk and look for villages along the train tracks. I need food, shelter, and work.*

*Have You Seen a Dark-Haired Man with Burning Eyes?* 77

Unfortunately, she was not welcomed in every village she passed through. Some peasants yelled profanities at her. Others threatened to hit her if she got closer or they actually kicked her. In one village, a woman pushed her so hard she fell and injured her back. She limped for days. No ear was there to hear her cry.

*Who am I to those people? Less important than a speck of dust.*

She felt sad, but it did not crush her spirit. She learned to slap back and to yell at men who made inappropriate advances to her. Fear never left her side, but she feared fewer things.

Adel had no choice but to keep looking for a friendlier welcome in the next village. When she found one, she would stay there for a while. She cleaned houses and animal pens. She was not always paid for her work. When she left a village to continue her journey, she saw herself as a lucky woman if she had a few rubles stuck in a sock, a loaf of bread, and a few apples smiling at her in her basket.

# 14
## Learning Geography by Foot

One day, while she was walking along the tracks, a train began to slow down. It was an opportunity she was not going to miss.

That was Adel's first time to jump onto a train but not the last. Usually, she had no money for a ticket. She hoped the trains she had snuck onto were going in the direction she needed. When on the train, she was forced to play hide-and-seek with conductors. She hid under benches at night. During the days, she balanced herself on the train shafts between two carriages. Nauseated by the shaking and rattling, she listened to the cha-ka-chaka-chaka-chaka- chaka of the train. She shivered from the freezing wind blowing between the shafts. She watched the ground underneath her disappear at frightening speed.

It took her several months, but she made it to Novosibirsk, unharmed.

The summer was over. Gray skies and an arctic wind sliced through her clothes and welcomed her as she stepped out of the train station. Winter announced its arrival.

The city was shrouded with dark clouds, reflected in the windows of Soviet-style tall and stark-looking buildings, clustered uniformly in gray. Overwhelming statues of Russian heroes were in every corner of the major streets seen from underneath the overpowering arch of the entrance to the train station. The city looked unfriendly and impenetrable.

Adel retreated to the station. It was warmer inside. She took off her head kerchief and put it in her basket. People poured out from incoming trains. Others pushed forward to get on time to trains leaving the station. No one had any regard for vagabonds like her. The corridors looked like long and dark bowels, ready to swallow those inside.

She had never seen so many people in one place. True, she had never been in Warsaw, but she had visited Zamosc, the Polish city closest to Izbica. Lvov was also a big city, but, by the crowds at the train station, she thought Novosibirsk must be much bigger.

Her initial thought was, *Where do I hide?* It was easy to get lost in the pushing and hurrying crowd, but what was the aim of being pushed and shoved? She had to find a place for the night. It was still light outside. Another Siberian wintry white night.

The safest places to hide were deep inside the station, far from the platforms, away from watching eyes and from other vagabonds. She found a nook and crouched against the wall. She felt warm. The air was condensed and sickening. She was hungry but had no food left in her basket or rubles in her sock.

*Hunger has no shame nor dignity, but it has excellent vision,* she thought.

And without any hesitation, she grabbed a half-eaten apple somebody had thrown on the ground. She wiped what was left of the apple and took slow and tiny bites, savoring every bite like a fine delicacy and as if there were a tomorrow.

Her last thought before she fell into yet another dreamless sleep was, *Itchale, where are you my love?*

Voices of a man and a woman speaking Yiddish woke her up. She was startled to see they were sitting not far from her. Eavesdropping, she understood they were a couple on their way from Mongolia to Moscow. Adel hesitated for a moment. Should she walk over to them? That would reveal her identity. Facing her fear head-on, she walked over.

*What do I have to lose? They may have information that will help me further.*

"A gitten morgen (good morning)," she greeted them in Yiddish. The woman looked startled.

"Forgive me. I didn't mean to scare you. I overheard you talking. I just arrived from the Urals, and I am looking for my husband."

The couple did not say a word. They looked at each other, deciding how to react to the strange woman. Could she be trusted? What was her story?

Adel could feel their trepidation. She would have had a similar reaction had she been approached by someone who looked and sounded like her.

Not to raise further suspicion, she did not ask what brought them to Mongolia or what got them out of there. Adel asked about Itchale—the dark-haired man. They had not seen him.

But, they assured her, "There are Jews all over Siberia and Mongolia, and even a Jewish office of sort in Novosibirsk."

Adel had never heard about Jews living in Mongolia. *What do they look like? What language do they speak? Will I be able to communicate with any?* she wondered.

*One thing at a time*, she thought. *I got the information I needed. It's time to look for the office they mentioned.*

She thanked them and walked out into the cold. It was daylight but still gray.

She found the "Jewish office." They could not help her in finding Itchale. But, like others before them, they advised her to stop searching or search someplace else—"Perhaps in Irkutsk or further east," they said. "It is only eighteen hundred kilometers away." All Adel heard was "Irkutsk!" The distance was meaningless. Distances were measured in time, the time it would take her to get to the next destination. She had no doubt she would get to Irkutsk. It was not a question of "how" but of "when." She was learning geography by foot.

She did not get much information at the office for Jewish affairs. But a compassionate woman who worked there surprised Adel by handing her a bowl of steaming soup and a big slice of bread. The woman watched Adel as she gulped down the soup, drinking the boiling liquid like tea and wiping off the last drop with the slice of bread. When Adel was done, the woman offered her a pair of thick felt gloves. She apologized to Adel that they were man's gloves.

"Their gender does not bother me," Adel said, thanking her and laughing.

Before Adel was ready to leave the office, she tried to put on the gloves. Something was stuck in the right glove.

"Unbelievable!" she exclaimed. Two rubles were stuffed in the fingers of the glove. Adel rushed over to the woman and showed her the glove and the two rubles.

"Please take it. It belongs to you," said the woman, smiling. "It's not mine. It is your lucky day. Take it."

"Are you sure?"

She nodded in approval and gestured with her hand to keep going.

*Thank God for that woman's menschlichkeit*, Adel thought. Adel walked back toward the train station. It was early afternoon. Walking in the street, she caught a glimpse of herself

in the display window of a store. She did not recognize herself, a Baba Yaga wearing layers of clothes, boots larger than her feet, her hands lost in huge gloves.

"But I look proportional. The size of my hands matches the size of my boots," she said aloud, laughing uncontrollably. With that appearance, even Itchale would not recognize her.

But she was warm now and not hungry, and that was all that mattered.

Whether walking in the street of a city, through a village, or in the taiga, Adel was focused, efficient, intense, and always alert to her surroundings. Her eyes caught a glimpse of a newspaper on the sidewalk, rolling in the wind. She ran and got it. The gloves were falling off her hands. If she stuffed them with paper, she thought, they would fit better, and she would feel warmer.

# 15
# On the Trans-Siberian Train

Adel failed to sneak onto the train. There were too many policemen around watching every platform, so she started walking along the tracks. She walked only a few kilometers when she heard a train slowing down. She imagined the train engineer slowed down especially for her.

*What did he see?* she wondered while chasing the train. *A skinny, rags-cladded woman walking alone in the icy wind? No time to think. Jump! Now!*

Where did she find the courage and strength to run alongside the train and grab on to an iron rod? She could feel the burning hot rod even through the thick felt of her gloves. With sheer willpower, she pulled herself into an open wagon. She hoped not to be caught by a conductor and that the train was going to Irkutsk. *I have lots of hopes*, she thought.

It was not meant to be a peaceful ride. She positioned herself in a corner, minimizing her presence for fear of getting attention. She took a bite of the stale bread she still had with her. The motion and the monotonous sounds of the fast-moving train put her to sleep. Her sleep was sweet perhaps but short. Somebody was shaking her shoulder. A man's voice was nudging her. "Get up! Get up!"

Startled, she jumped to her feet.

"Get your hands off me!" she yelled, ready to slap him.

The man who shook her shoulder took a step back in surprise. Another man said in a husky voice, "Don't get excited, blondie. We are friendly guys."

She grabbed her basket and moved closer to the exit door. She looked at them. Two tramps reeking of cheap alcohol, with disheveled beards, woolen caps, and in a mishmash of military uniform, stared at her. Wobbling from one foot to the other, they tried to balance themselves in the moving train.

"Hey, who are you?" demanded the first drifter who had shaken her shoulder. His buddy shoved himself closer to Adel, trying to unbutton her coat. She could smell his bad breath. Adel slapped his hand. It did not deter him. On the contrary, her slap excited him. He pushed himself a bit closer.

"We found us a spirited blondie," he yelled victoriously. The first one, encouraged by his comrade, was getting ready to grab her.

Adel froze for a split second.

*They'll kill me if I stay*, she thought. *The train is slowing down. Jump, Adel! Jump! Now!*

And she jumped. Amazingly, she did not break her legs. She was only bruised.

That would not be the last time on her journey she would barely escape men who tried to harm her.

Adel stayed for the rest of the night where she fell. Too injured to walk, too shaken to wander away from the tracks. Her body was injured; her spirit, though, was not.

She felt proud for remaining clean and untouched. *I am keeping myself for one man—my Itchale. Nothing is going to change that.*

At daylight, she noticed a sign in the near distance. "Zima."

She found odd jobs in Zima that enabled her to survive through the winter. She didn't meet any Jews. Although no one knew about gulags in the area, she was advised to continue farther to the southeast—to the city of Irkutsk. Zima was only two hundred and forty kilometers away, she was told.

"Only." *What a small distance*, she thought. A distance unimaginable yesterday was doable today. She shook her head in disbelief. *Adel, Adel, what became of you? When did you become such a "molodyets" (a brave guy)?* She noticed: the language of her heart was Yiddish. The language of her courage became Russian.

# 16
# "Too Kitchy"

Adel crossed the wilderness of the Siberian taiga. She was heading to Irkutsk.

In the taiga, she was afraid of the four-legged animals of the forests and of the two-legged who lived in the villages. Occasionally, she met good people, like a villager with a horse and buggy, who gave her a ride. Or someone else, who handed her something to eat. She ate whatever she foraged from the fields—food of the sort that gave her constant bellyaches.

While walking through the taiga forest, along the Trans-Siberian train tracks, she saw dozens of small cemeteries, like colorful dots tucked away in the woods. Villagers built gravesites and headstones in different shapes—rectangle, triangle, and crosses. The graves were decorated with colorful ribbons and flowers. Some had pictures of the deceased on them. Those gave her an eerie feeling when she walked by. As if ghosts were watching her.

After days of walking, she arrived in Irkutsk, a city on hills in the midst of the taiga forest.

Adel walked along the banks of the Angara River. She was impressed by the colorful gardens and statues, the bridges over the mighty river, and the industrial buildings around. She made it to midtown. A heart-shaped gate made of red roses caught her attention. *Wouldn't that be a beautiful place to take a picture with Itchale?* She dismissed the thought immediately. *He wouldn't like that. It was too kitchy.*

She walked the streets, searching for one familiar face—that of Itchale, of course.

She was listening for Yiddish, for a familiar Polish accent, for a hint. She found the market and even an office for Jewish affairs. Itchale was nowhere to be found.

She kept gathering information.

"Far away from Irkutsk, perhaps in Mongolia or even as far as in Vladivostok, there are gulags," she was told.

Was that information truthful? Or was it fear that drove people to distance her, the asking-stranger, she often wondered.

She had no way of telling. There was only one choice left. To keep going in the direction pointed.

The winter was brutally cold. The temperature dropped to minus forty, and with the arctic wind blowing, it felt even lower than that.

The office for Jewish affairs let her stay there during the nights. Their kitchen provided her with a meal a day. In return, she cleaned the offices and helped in the kitchen.

The winter was about to be over. When the snow started melting and the wind had calmed down, she was ready to continue her journey.

She had saved a few rubles; she had food and a pair of men's boots, which someone gave her out of pity. The boots were too big for her feet and too heavy. But they were sturdy and she had no better ones anyway.

*I am used to the "babushka" look,* she thought. *I wonder if I'll ever look pretty, like a young woman again? Ah, foolish thoughts of a feeble mind.*

# 17
# "It Is So Beautiful"

She heard about Lake Baikal.

It was less than three hundred kilometers from Irkutsk. People talked about the beauty of "the largest and deepest freshwater lake in the world."

They described the beautiful country cottages, the "dachas," which wealthy Russians held as vacation homes near the lake. The cottages, they said, were surrounded by rich vegetable gardens, trees bent over with red delicious apples, flowers of all colors and shapes. And in the spring, all is wrapped in the intoxicating scents of jasmine and lilac in full bloom.

*What descriptions!* She shook her head. It was beyond her imagination.

Although her journey had a mission, it was also a trip to a world new to her. Adel was eager to see and smell that beauty. Lake Baikal was going to be on her way farther east and south to Mongolia. She walked close to the Trans-Siberian train tracks. The days were getting longer and warmer. Spring was in the air, and she could take off her heavy coat.

The taiga was waking up after a long winter nap. It was rejoicing with no care for the rest of the world that was on fire.

Adel's head was spinning. She felt dizzy just by looking at the hundreds of flowers in vibrant colors of yellow, red, orange, white, and purple. She envied the butterflies and crickets, humming and buzzing, bubbling in happy rhythms, with no worry for tomorrow.

*Nature is like a self-absorbed person, indifferent to anything or anybody outside him*, she thought.

Spring was celebrating, but she felt like an outsider, like an uninvited guest who peeks into a dacha he will never be invited to. *What do I have to do with all that richness*, she thought, *with that beauty of nature which is completely oblivious to my aching heart?*

One day, as she was walking along the railroad tracks, a slow-moving train passed by. She hopped on it.

She was on the train only a few hours when she saw from a distance a huge, elongated blue "eye," surrounded by the evergreen of the taiga forest. It was the legendary Lake Baikal. She was excited when the train announced its arrival at the Baikal station.

Without any warning, she felt a heavy hand on her shoulder, a shove and a kick, and next, she found herself flying straight into the icy water of the blue eye. The freezing water almost took her breath. Her scream froze in midair as her body hit the water. The sadistic laughter of the conductor who pushed her echoed in her ears for days. It felt like a burn in her heart.

She dragged herself out of the water with some effort and sat down on a rock. She was shivering in her wet clothes, her heart about to explode.

She checked her legs and arms. No bruises. Not visible ones anyway.

*I am fine. I'll survive*, she assured herself.

She calmed down, breathing easier.

It was quiet and peaceful. The blue sky reflected in the crystal clear water and multiplied itself in a million sparkling tiny mirrors. Colorful flowers carpeted the banks of the lake and even the dense forest looked friendly. Adel sat on the bank, soaking in the warmth radiated from the rocks. Her eyes slowly caressed all that surrounded her. Watching in awe, she felt as if enclosed in a bubble. For a fleeting moment, detached from fear and worry, and even from longings, she felt the essence of beauty.

"It is so beautiful," she whispered.

Beauty aside, the ever-down-to-earth Adel decided to take another dip in the icy water since she was wet already.

*I had better rinse my hair and my "shmattes" (rags) as long as the sun is still out. And if I have any lice, the cold water will take their breath away as well as mine*, she thought.

Before she took her clothes off, she looked around to check for wandering eyes. It was safe. She picked some dry weeds and smashed them in her fist, the way she learned from peasants during her travel across Siberia.

This would make good "soap." She walked into the water, careful not to fall on the slippery rocks. She giggled in delight when tiny fish nibbled on her bare feet.

She washed her hair and body. The scrubbing felt so good, she moaned loudly, forgetting that wandering eyes usually have listening ears attached to them.

She rinsed her socks, her dresses, her head kerchief, and her underwear. She spread her clothes to dry on the warm rocks. When she was done, before completely drying, she put on her slip, the one she bought for her wedding—the most delicate garment she ever owned. She wore it mainly for practical and not senti-mental reasons—it kept her warm.

The day was warm and windy, and her clothes dried fast. It felt good to wear her clean clothes again. If she could only find something to eat.

She climbed over the bank and walked toward the train station.

There, near the tracks, was a hut. She could see someone was watching her through a crack in a window. She walked over but felt reluctant to knock on the door. What should she say to the woman watching her?

The door opened and an old woman came out. She was a true Siberian babushka. Adel was amazed to see the layers of long dresses the babushka was wearing. Once colorful, now faded, she wore a head kerchief, dark woolen socks, and man's shoes.

Even in such an uncertain situation, Adel did not lose her sense of humor.

*I can learn from her how to improve my Baba Yaga attire,* she thought.

The babushka said, "Take it, my child."

To Adel's amazement, she handed her a cup of hot tea and a slice of bread.

"Eat and may God bless you."

Adel was in tears. How could she expect that? She took the babushka's hand and kissed it in gratitude.

*Go figure, life*, she thought. *A minute earlier, a man tried to kill me; a minute later, an angel saves my life. A miracle? Compassion. Menschlichkeit!*

As she was walking away toward the train station, the babushka called her back.

"Take the blanket my child. The nights are cold here."

Adel was speechless.

"Da svidania (Thank you)."

She blessed the babushka again in the names of all the saints she knew and walked back to the station for the night. She curled up on a bench and covered herself with the blanket. With food in her belly and warmth in her heart, she waited for a new day.

She woke up with the arrival of a train. Without anyone around to see, she snuck onto the train going east and off she went toward Mongolia.

# 18

# "Shooing" a Yak in Mongolia

The train stopped.

"Are we in Mongolia?" she asked a passenger.

"No. We are in Ulan-Ude, still in Russia, but close to the Mongolian border."

*I'll better get off,* she decided. *It is a city. I'll find people to ask about Itchale or gulags.*

She jumped off the train before any conductor discovered her.

She walked into the city of Ulan-Ude. Only one hundred kilometers from Lake Baikal but worlds apart.

She walked around, dazed by the wonders of the city. It was the first time she saw Buryats—tribal people in a variety of ethnic outfits, speaking an unfamiliar language. She, who never heard of Buddhism or Tibet, learned this city was the center of Tibetan Buddhism. She met Tatars and mistook them for Chinese. The Buddhist temples, she thought, were more beautiful than the churches. She wandered to the Red Gate on Lenin Street. The gate marked the road to Mongolia and to China. Neighboring China, she heard, was only three thousand kilometers away. The same road west led to Novosibirsk. All transports of prisoners sent to gulags went through the Red Gate.

*Did Itchale go through this gate to Mongolia?* she wondered. She stood under the arch for a long time. Which direction should she take? Back to Novosibirsk? Or further east and south to Mongolia?

People suggested Mongolia. She had explored the Novosibirsk area already or so she thought. *Mongolia then.*

By foot, by train, by bus, and with anyone who gave her a ride—she crossed the Mongolian mountains and the Gobi Desert.

And one day, still on a train, she opened her eyes to see a city. "I, Adel, from the shtetl, am in Mongolia! And in the capital Ulaanbaatar!" she cried out.

Even in her wildest dreams, she could not have imagined such a big and colorful city. She got off the train and walked around as if she was in a dream.

For some unknown reason, she felt instantly at home in the big city.

Although it was a city in most parts, it looked like a big village.

While getting to know the city, she learned that in the Mongolian language, Ulaanbaatar meant "Red Hero." The enormous main square, which was named after Genghis Khan, the founder of the Mongol Empire, and the huge statues of all the Khans and their dynasty all made her feel like a little girl in wonderland.

She recalled seeing a picture once of a camel with one hump; here, to her surprise, she saw a camel with two humps. There were square and tall buildings like in any other city, but in this big city, people lived also in roundish tents—a yurt or a "ger," as the locals called it. And the music? Monotonic melodies, in guttural voices, like those she had heard not long ago in Ulan-Ude from Tibetan monks. She walked the streets, taking in the smells of animals mixed with people's sweat and spices, smells that were appealing and repulsive at the same time. She asked about Izak. The few who spoke Russian did not know of gulags or anyone who might have looked or sounded like Izak.

She could hardly see any of the secret police officers in the streets. Perhaps, for that reason, she felt almost like a free person since she had left Lvov.

If no Itchale, then she had to find a place to stay and work before she figured out where to go next.

She felt dizzy after walking for hours without eating. She leaned against a wall of a grocery store to catch her breath. She took off her head kerchief to wipe the sweat off her flushed face. The shopkeeper noticed her. A foreign young woman is going to faint at my doorstep. Do I need trouble, he thought, and, nevertheless, rushed to bring her a glass of water. The cold water brought her back to life.

"Which way is the marketplace?" she asked him.

He pointed straight ahead.

At the market, she met a Mongolian woman who was selling from a small stand vegetables, cheeses, and eggs. It was the crying of the woman's toddler which got Adel's attention. She walked over and smiled to the mother first, so she wouldn't be scared of her, then she smiled at the child.

"Ne plach (don't cry)," she said to him in Russian. Her smiling face and soft voice, spoken in a foreign language by a strange-looking woman, unlike his mother—stopped the child from crying. With his little mouth open, he seemed curious, not afraid. The toddler looked like a doll with his rosy-round cheeks, slanted black eyes, and with his little black hat and colorful outfit.

Adel shook the mother's hand. "I am Adel," she said.

"I am Batbayar," she responded in Russian, with a wide smile.

Adel repeated the name. "Bat-ba-yar." The name sounded foreign but pleasant. "What does it mean?"

"Batbayar means 'happiness.'" "And 'Adel'? What does that mean?" "Gentleness."

Happiness and gentleness enjoyed the poetic exchange of information. To the mother's delight, the child decided to climb into Adel's arms. They both laughed. Adel cradled him for a little bit, and within minutes, he fell asleep. Trust was asserted.

*I like them both*, she thought.

Batbayar complimented Adel. "You are good with children. Do you have any?"

Adel was quick to respond. "No. I am a newlywed, but I love children, and I can be very good at helping you here or at your home."

She saw an opportunity to find work and perhaps a place to stay.

*Shame is a luxury for a desperate person*, she said to herself. *I cannot afford any luxury now.*

Batbayar smiled. It so happened she had complained to her husband the other night that she needed help at her stand and at home. "Our boy is a handful. And I cannot take care of him and sell my merchandise all at the same time," she told him.

"Don't forget that I grow those vegetables and raise the chicken for your eggs, not to mention our yak!" He reminded her without his work, she would not have her work.

When Batbayar heard Adel's offer, she smiled to herself. *This woman is godsent*, she thought. *She looks clean and decent. I'll bring her home. She'll live with us, and she'll help me in the market and at home.*

Adel felt the shift in the woman's thoughts. In a slight sigh of relief, she put the sleepy toddler in his mother's arms.

"Where are you from?" asked Batbayar.

"I am from Poland, but I have lived in Russia for a while. I am looking for my husband. He disappeared on his way to work. I was told he might be in this area."

That was the story she told Batbayar.

Both women were probably close in age. It was hard to tell—Adel looked older, because of her babushka outfit—heavy men's boots, a head kerchief that used to be colorful, a winter coat, and a patched dress in faded colors from walking for days in the burning sun and scrubbed by dry grass instead of soap. Compared to the babushka, the Mongolian looked like a peacock in her tribal attire—a red felt hat, several skirts in vibrant colors, a black vest, matching woman's boots, and a colorful shawl over her shoulders.

Batbayar looked young and cheerful.

"If you are willing to work, I'll give you work, here and in my house. Today, you will come to us. I have a husband, and this one is our only child."

She shared with Adel the conversation she had with her husband a day earlier.

Adel thanked her profusely.

"I promise you will never regret this."

A bond was formed.

Their home was about an hour's walk from the market. Both women packed their baskets with the merchandise that did not sell, put the sleepy kid in a handmade stroller, and off they went "home." The small family lived in the outskirts of the city and, like all their neighbors, they lived in a yurt.

Batbayar's husband was as friendly as his wife. He was a Tatar. Short and stocky, with a smooth face and a thin mustache in an upside down "u" shape. Both father and his two-year-old son were named Altantsetseg. Adel, who could not pronounce their names without the risk of breaking her teeth, called the father "Big Alter" and the boy "Little Alter." Had they only known that Alter is a Jewish name, which means "old" in Yiddish, she smiled to herself. This was a private joke she was not going to share with them.

Is he a Tatar Jew she asked herself, looking at the yarmulke Big Alter was wearing. That, she found out, was a Mongolian man's traditional head cover.

He was a quiet man who did not speak much.

The love and respect between the couple were evident but their expressions subtle. He trusted his wife's judgment and did not ask Adel any questions. To make her feel welcomed in their home, and not as an outsider, the couple spoke Russian in front of her. That way she could also participate in conversation. The yurt was large enough to allow Adel some privacy by separating it with a curtain.

Adel did not sleep much the first night. The new adventure, the sounds and smells, and the presence of some big animal outside the yurt kept her awake until dawn.

In the morning, right after breakfast (bread, cheese made of yak's milk, and a cup of tea), the husband introduced her to the other "members" of their family who stayed in a shack attached to the yurt—a female yak and its baby "yakie."

She screamed when she first saw the yak. She had never seen or heard of such a beast. *Although the little one, like many little ones, is cute*, she thought.

One morning, Adel was busy cleaning the yurt when she heard some commotion from the vegetable garden outside. She moved the curtain a bit and looked outside. What she saw was both amusing and frightening. The yak had let itself out of the shed with its yakie and, with the confidence of massive animals that own the world, walked into the small vegetable garden. Adel looked on helplessly as the yak and its offspring trampled over everything that poked out of the hard soil and helped themselves to a feast of their favorite vegetables and a few flowers as well.

Adel tried to "shoo" the yaks away. Mother and giant baby were completely oblivious to her "shooing." When she told Batbayar and the two Alters about the event, all had a big laugh—"Shooing" a yak?

Adel lived with the family, helped with the child and the house chores. She attended the garden when the husband was busy with his other jobs and churned butter from the yak's milk but kept a respectful distance from the yaks. She learned to speak the local language and sing their songs. They spent many evenings singing. Older Alter played a few musical instruments. The neighbors joined in, especially on winter nights. They respected her solitude and never suggested she forget her husband or find a "replacement" man. Adel was treated with great respect and affection. She joined them in their festivities and when they wandered to the mountains to visit relatives. She even drove with them to the Gobi Desert to visit a shaman. All was new to her and exciting. She adjusted well to her life there, but she never forgot the reason she was in Mongolia—to gather information, regain her strength and the means to continue her search for her Itchale.

She used every opportunity to ask about Izak and gulags. No one knew or had seen him.

And about gulags? "Go farther east and south to Vladivostok," she was told. "There is a big gulag there."

She loved that Mongolian family, but almost a year later, the day came when she had to move on. The small family—Batbayar was pregnant now—walked her to the train station. Adel bought a ticket to Vladivostok.

# 19

# Reaching the Edge
# of the Continent

If you go farther, you would fall into the Sea of Japan or into the Pacific Ocean," she was told.

Vladivostok, "The Ruler of the East" as it was called, was a city located on the edge of Russia's Far East. It took the train only forty-eight hours to zip the thirty-nine hundred kilometers to get to its last stop. Adel did not understand why there were so many military men on the train. And why she was the only civilian who got off at the Vladivostok station. She was told in Ulaanbaatar there was a "big gulag" in the Vladivostok area. But where was it?

All her questions were answered very quickly. Vladivostok was the main naval base for the Soviet Pacific Fleet. The entire city was closed to foreigners and visitors.

She wondered why she had been told to go there? Didn't these people know they were sending her to a guarded military area where she would be arrested if she dared to ask about a missing person and gulags? Those kinds of questions were dangerous and forbidden anywhere in Russia in those times.

"Oy to my life!" cried Adel. "What should I do now? Where should I go from here?"

She had reached the end of Russia. She was at the edge of the Asian continent.

Adel had crossed two continents, and her journey was not over yet.

She stayed at the train station, hoping to get on another train that went back—west. But where to?

Then it suddenly dawned on her. *I have been "schlepping (wandering)" around for three years! How did time fly? Was I asleep?*

A train arrived. Where should she go? All the way back to the same places? No. She would go south. To wherever she had not been yet.

*I have to buy a ticket. What should I say my destination is without raising suspicion?* she thought.

*The train is going to Mongolia, to Ulaanbaatar.*

*I am going back to Mongolia then.*

Going back—to the west, south, and north.

Forty-eight hours later, she arrived in the capital Ulaanbaatar. Just in time.

Adel had very little money left for another ticket or for food. Security was not tight at the station, so she snuck onto another train. She did not care whether it went west or south as long as she was heading toward a city.

She was on the Trans-Siberian train for days or perhaps weeks. She lost track of time. The train crossed majestic vistas of mountains, forests, and rivers. But who could enjoy the ride when she had to play hide-and-seek with conductors and suspicious passengers?

She was caught, again. This time she was lucky to be kicked off at a stop, not when the train was still moving.

# GOING BACK—
# TO THE
# WEST, SOUTH
# AND NORTH

# 20
# Running As Fast As She Can

She did not know she could run so fast. Away from a policeman who was chasing her, she ran toward a city.

She found herself in Alma-Ata, in Kazakhstan. She could not believe it! She learned she was thirty-four hundred kilometers further south from Mongolia.

When she was already inside the city and far away from the chasing policeman, she asked herself, *What reason do I have to feel happy? But I am.* The weather was warm. The city looked bubbly, full of life. A whole new adventure was awaiting her. Perhaps Itchale would be there.

As she did in every city, she walked around, learning the city, listening to people, watching out for policemen, searching for fellow Jews. She was surprised to see mosques and people who looked like Mongolians. They wore ethnic clothes and colorful yarmulkes. These were Muslim. She heard Russian and many other dialects she had never heard before. Very quickly, she found the bazaar. That was the place to ask questions and to look for a familiar face or language.

Itchale was not there either, and Adel ended up staying in Alma-Ata several months. She worked cleaning houses, sweeping the streets, and in any other odd job that paid by cash or food. And she found a place to stay.

She met a few Jewish people who told her she had been misled. "There was a gulag," they said. "But near the Ural Mountains, north of Novosibirsk, and closer to the city of Omsk."

"'Near' means hundreds of kilometers or thousands?" she asked, as if it made a difference.

There was a gulag! And close to the area she had visited a long time ago. Her heart was about to jump out of her chest.

*I must be crazy!* she thought. *Instead of discouragement, I feel encouraged. I have a new destination—the Ural, Novosibirsk, Omsk, and hope. I cannot wait to get on the road again.*

# 21
## Laughing Her Ribs Off

And off she went—by foot, by train, and by whatever and with whoever gave her a ride.

She had food in her basket, better boots, and a couple of colorful dresses she got from her landlady in Alma-Ata. She got the dresses as an exchange for her wedding slip.

One day, when Adel was hanging her landlady's laundry, she added her own washed laundry, including her slip. Although clean, years of wear had changed its color from white to a grayish-yellow. The color did not deter Adel's landlady (she liked to be called "Madame Landlady") from wanting it. There was no point in arguing with her. That used, grayish-yellow "shmatte" (rag) looked attractive to her. She desired it, and in exchange, she offered Adel two new dresses. Adel would have given her the slip for free.

"Why do you need that slip?" Adel asked.

Madame Landlady and her husband were peasants who had moved to the big city because of the husband's position in the Communist Party. He was climbing the party ladder. As an important couple, they were invited to parties. The madame thought Adel's slip would make the perfect ball gown. Adel tried to talk her out of it. She told her it was an undergarment, not a ball gown. Her explanations fell on deaf ears. Happy like a child, Madame Landlady took the slip and pulled it over her clothes.

Ignoring her protests, she dragged Adel to a "tango" around the yard. One woman giggling, perfectly happy; the other, laughing her ribs off.

Madame Landlady wore the slip at the ball. She was the "queen of the ball"—the subject of envy of all the other dancing women. But Adel never wore the dresses she was given.

*I will not be caught dead in those dresses*, she said to herself, laughing. *To look like a babushka is one thing; to look like a folk dancer is a whole different story. I am not ready for that yet. Or ever.*

Adel left Alma-Ata and went back to the Urals and Novosibirsk. En route to the southern Urals, she arrived in Jambyl, a city on the Talas River, one of the oldest cities of Kazakhstan. Although it was a pretty city, with its snow-capped mountains on the horizon and ancient mosques, she did not feel comfortable there. She was appalled by the local habit of spitting in the streets. She recoiled from drunk men lying on sidewalks everywhere she looked. Adel left that place as fast as she could.

# 22
# Singing "Kalinka, Malinka"

From Jambyl, in the low range mountains of Kazakhstan, across the higher range, she went on to the Ural Mountains for the second time.

It was still warm when Adel returned to Siberia, about twenty-three hundred kilometers away, give or take a few hundred.

She wandered around the Urals asking about a gulag. The only information she got was, "There is a chance to find something closer to Novosibirsk or Omsk."

She got on the Trans-Siberian train when she managed to sneak on. And off the train when she was forced to.

One of those trains took her to Novosibirsk.

Now, the second time in Novosibirsk, almost five years had passed.

It was a dreary, gray, and cold morning when Adel arrived in Novosibirsk. *Does the sun ever shine here?* she wondered.

She was walking in the bowels of the train station when she suddenly heard music. The music poured from outside the station into its dimly lit hallways.

*I have to see where it comes from. Who plays and for whom?* she wondered. This time, she knew the whereabouts of the station and, therefore, was less frightened. She skipped toward the music.

In a light drizzle, under the massive arched entrance of the train station, some dignitaries, important passengers of the Trans-Siberian train, were welcomed with song and dance. Musicians were playing Russian folk songs on their accordions and balalaikas. Dancers swirled around the square in vibrant costumes like huge, colorful butterflies brightening the grayness of the city. And singers with beautiful, crystal voices penetrated the hearts. The songs told stories of lost loves, of lovers separated by wars, and of longings to the vast horizons of Mother Russia. Adel tapped her foot to the music. She knew the words to most of the songs and was deeply moved.

Tears in her eyes and careful not to be heard, she quietly joined the singers. "Malinka, Kalinka, Malinka Moya."

Adel walked away. It became dangerous to stay in one place for too long. She knew how to disappear in a crowd. She would have to come back to the station for the night. Meanwhile, she could not waste any time. This time, she knew what to ask about gulags. And more important, how to listen to what was said between the lines.

She heard rumors there was a lumber "operation" near the city of Omsk. An operation meant a labor camp or a prison. *But how near was "near"?* Omsk was about six hundred kilometers north of Novosibirsk, she was told. *Can I make it in the wintertime?* she asked herself the obvious question. *Should I find a place to stay for the winter in Novosibirsk? Where?*

The thought that Itchale might be in that area forced her to take the risk and start walking toward Omsk.

If she only had the money for a train ticket, it would have taken her about eight hours to get there. But since she had none, Adel had no choice but to walk. Almost a month's walk.

# 23
## "Those Eyes"

Adel never made it to Omsk. The winter was almost over, but it was still brutally cold. The snow was deep, and it had not melted yet.

The soles of her boots had worn-out. By now, they had more holes than soles left. She had to wrap her feet with rags but to no avail. Her feet were injured and her toes frozen.

She dragged herself from village to village along the train tracks and away from them. She met other vagabonds like her. Rarely did she meet a man walking alone and never a woman walking by herself. When she was asked what she was doing in the taiga by herself, she'd answer with a question. She was always careful to ask about Izak and the way to a gulag. She never fully trusted anybody. Usually, people exchanged very few words.

She learned that fear was the ruler. Silence was the rule in the woods.

One day started like any other day, but that one day ended differently.

As she made her way through the forest, falling into the knee-high snow, she felt that her heart was pulling her in a certain direction.

She always listened to her heart—it was both her conscience and her compass.

Blinded by the whiteness of the snow, Adel was startled to discover she almost tripped over a broken wooden fence.

*Why is there a fence in the depth of the forest?* There was no sign of people living in the wilderness. *What does the fence protect?*

The thought crossed her mind. Then from a distance, she suddenly saw barracks.

*How is that possible? In the middle of nowhere? Who lives here? Am I imagining? Do the hunger and the bleached snow finally trick my mind? It must be a mirage. Nobody can live here—but the fence is real.*

She kept walking toward the mirage, drawn to it uncontrollably. She had to find out. The only sounds she heard were her heartbeat and the swish-swash of her labored steps. She was not hallucinating. It was a fence, and those were barracks. She stopped to calm down her racing heart. She pushed the fence. Another board fell down.

*I cannot believe my eyes! A camp?* she squinted.

The barracks—like black rocks thrown by an unknown hand on a white carpet—were still there. She walked through the gap straight into a camp.

*A labor camp! Oh my god, where am I? When will the guards show up?*

Her heart was about to explode from fear and anticipation. No guards.

*Am I in the lumber "operation"? The gulag?*

And then she saw the man. He was staring at her.

*Where did he come from? He does not look like a guard. How long has he been staring at me?* She grabbed her chest.

*Those eyes!*

The man was holding a cigarette in the palm of his left hand—protecting the cigarette from the wind. She recognized that typical gesture and she knew those eyes.

*Itchale?!*

# IN THE GULAG—A NEW REALITY

# 24

## Yossale

It was the beginning of winter in 1940. Izak went to the marketplace in Lvov to sell a down blanket.

He left home with a heavy heart, telling his wife that if he did not come back, she needed to take good care of herself. He never made it back. He was abducted by the Red Army soldiers who were on a hunt for laborers for coal mines, kolkhozes—collective farms, and gulags—forced labor camps and prisons. The captured were transported into trucks that took them to places with no return—to gulags in Siberia or to remote kolkhozes, across the two continents, Europe and Asian Russia.

While Itchale was settling in, against his will, in his new life in the Siberian gulag, his wife took matters in her hands and started a search for him that took her across two continents.

He gave up seeing her again. She never gave up finding him.

One evening, while walking to his barrack back from the communal shower, he heard someone calling him. "Itchale." Not "Izak"—"Itchale."

He turned around toward the voice, but he could not see anybody. All he wanted after twelve hours of logging trees was a shower, a cigarette, and food. Since he had taken a shower already, and he devoured the seven hundred grams of bread he was given, there was nothing else for him to do but to collapse on his mattress for another dreamless night. He was not in any mood for surprises.

"Itchale!" The voice sounded urgent now.

Who was calling him? He had been only a few days at the camp. Who would know his nickname—"Itchale"? It must be somebody from the shtetl. From Izbica!

He looked around again. This time, he noticed about ten meters away from him, an older man in an oversized hooded coat, standing attached to the wall of a barrack. The hood covered most of his face. The man looked planted in the ground in his heavy boots. Itchale strained his eyes to see, but he could not recognize the man.

"Who are you?"

The man took a step forward. "Itchale, it's me. Yossale from Izbica! Don't you recognize me?"

The man was standing now in front of him, smiling. He was toothless. Itchale was not sure yet.

But then he saw the smile in his eyes, and he recognized him at once. "Yossale!"

His childhood friend from the shtetl. His best friend for adventures and other mischiefs and the one who competed with him for Adel's heart, as if he ever had a chance.

Itchale was shocked to see his friend's condition. His eyes and lips were sunken. He had lost his teeth! *What happened to him? Dare I ask? He is my age!* Watching Itchale's expression, Yossale guessed what went through his friend's mind.

"Itchale, I don't want to scare you. But this is what hunger and hard labor will do to you. I am lucky to be alive."

*If he is "lucky," who is "unlucky"? Is this what I have to look forward to?* he thought bitterly.

"Yossale! When did you arrive? Let's go inside," he suggested.

The men walked toward Itchale's barrack. It was too cold to stand outside after a shower. And besides, sooner or later, a guard would "entice" them with his rifle-butt to seek shelter anyway.

"You don't want to know," Yossale said. "I was caught by a policeman in a store in Novosibirsk while helping myself to a jar of herring. Can you imagine? A pauper's dream—to taste a slice of herring one more time, even if my life depended on it. The policeman announced that I was 'a leech and a parasite—an enemy of the people' and sent me to be 'reeducated' in this gulag. This happened about six years ago. I have been reeducated here since."

Both men laughed. Neither could be reeducated or so they thought. Hunger and terror, they found out, were superb educators even for spirited fellows like Itchale and Yossale.

"How did you end up here?" asked Yossale. "Is Adel with you?"

*He sounds too hopeful,* thought Itchale. "No. Adel is in Lvov. Let me tell you my sad story."

"Tell him some other time!" yelled somebody in the barrack. "We want to sleep!"

*There is no point in arguing,* thought Itchale. *Who knows how long I'll have to stay with these men? Better not to make enemies.* He knew that barking dogs do bite sometimes.

"Let's talk tomorrow," said Yossale.

They hugged, patting each other on the back. Yossale left for his barrack, and Itchale dove into the bottomless depth of a dreamless sleep.

The morning siren woke him up for another day of logging trees. However, that day was going to be different. Yossale was there, and they were going to rekindle their friendship.

*All is good,* thought Itchale, *although I am not sure I will get used to his toothless smile. Poor devil.* He smiled while checking his teeth with his tongue. Cynicism was not foreign to him, but he truly liked the "poor devil."

*How little one needs to turn despair into hope,* he thought.

Exactly twelve hours later, after the evening meal—soup, bread, and something gray that smelled like fish—was served; after a shower and a smoke, he walked over to Yossale's barrack. His friend was waiting for him, eager for conversation. Yossale sat on his double mattress. He was long enough in the gulag to find his way around for an extra mattress. He pulled out the second mattress and put it in front of his. Itchale sat down facing his friend. *Although they have better "furniture," their barrack is definitely filthier than ours,* thought Itchale. *But if it does not bother Yossale, why should it bother me?*

Anyway, the veterans in Yossale's barrack were less enthusiastic than the newcomers in Itchale's barrack. They seemed apathetic enough to allow a conversation.

# 25
## Misery Loves Company

"So, tell me, what happened to you? Why is Adel in Lvov and you are not with her?" asked Yossale.

He was curious to hear Itchale's story, and Itchale was eager to tell. It was the first time he felt safe enough to share his story, the story he wanted to tell his wife.

"All happened on a Tuesday morning a few weeks ago. I had gone to the bazaar almost every day since we arrived in Lvov from Izbica. I was looking for work, but I could not find any. So we decided to sell a down blanket we brought with us from home.

"There were rumors that Jews were kidnapped by the Russian army or police and sent away to labor camps. We had hoped in Lvov we would find some peace, but there was no peace anywhere.

"That morning, I woke up with a bad feeling. I did not want to scare Adel, but she sensed that something was wrong. I decided to go to the bazaar anyway, but I was worried about her. So I told her that if I didn't come back home, she should take good care of herself."

"What's wrong with you? That's what you told your wife so she wouldn't be worried?" Yossale shook his head. "And I thought you were the smarter one between us."

"What can I say? I was an idiot. I didn't think. She begged me not to go. I'm afraid she ran after me. It was too late. I had to go. We had to eat.

"So, I left, and I never made it back. I did not even have a chance to show my merchandise yet when military trucks pulled into the marketplace and blocked all surrounding streets.

"There was no way to turn around and escape. Within minutes, the marketplace was full of soldiers and police officers. I knew I was in trouble when they started ordering all those who signed up for work in the coal mines to come forward. I did not sign up, but it did not matter to the soldiers. The soldiers dragged everyone who appeared suspicious to them. In other words, all Jews or other minorities—mostly men but even women with children. I was included among the suspicious. Actually, I was told later that what raised their suspicion was my looks and my Russian. To them, I looked like a Russian Muslim from one of their Asian states, but since my Russian was 'too good' for an Uzbek or a Kazakh, I 'must have been a spy.' My explanations of why I was at the bazaar fell on deaf ears. It was clear they came to clean out the area from 'negative elements,' or simply put, Mother Russia needed laborers for the war effort. Who was I to resist the Mother?" He smiled bitterly.

"Dozens of men and women with children were loaded into trucks. Each was assigned to a truck and was given a number. Mine was truck 'A' and the 'lucky' number—thirteen. From that moment on, we were 'numbers'—not individuals with any human rights."

"Tell me about those 'human rights,'" said Yossale in self-righteousness, interrupting Itchale's flow. He had forgotten he was in the gulag because he was caught stealing.

"Needless to say, under those circumstances, it was impossible to leave a message for Adel. We were not told where we were being taken or why. The trucks drove us to the train station in Lvov. Not a passenger train but a special train with cattle wagons was already waiting for us. Inside each wagon were several decks of wooden benches, built one above the other. In our wagon, there was room for thirty men, perhaps. They managed to cram in sixty to seventy. It was so overcrowded we could not sit straight. In one corner of the wagon was a hole made to 'relieve our natural needs.' With no privacy, it was humiliating to use the hole. The air was stuffy and nauseating. Adults, like children, were crying and arguing. All terrified. In the middle of the wagon, there was an iron stove that was not burning. It was supposed to be fed by coal, but we did not get any coal."

Yossale shook his head. "You had it worse than I did in the prisoners' train. We were cramped into cattle wagons, but it was not so crowded, and we were at least fed."

"I'm tired," said Itchale. "I'll see you tomorrow." Reliving his journey brought up other painful memories—his worry about Adel and his family in Izbica and in Lvov. He was not ready to share those thoughts yet.

He took off the clean prisoner's uniform he wore after the shower and put it neatly on the concrete floor next to his mattress. He was going to wear it for work tomorrow. He pulled out from the basket he brought with him from Lvov (a few pieces of the down blanket were still there) a pair of civilian pants, a reminder of more hopeful days, and a woolen shirt—and put them on for sleep.

He pulled the itchy woolen blanket over his head and tried to sleep. The natural sounds and smells discharged by the men sleeping were like a rude awakening that it was not a nightmare he would wake from.

*Can I live in a herd and not become part of the cattle? Will I survive?* Those were his last thoughts before he fell asleep.

# 26
## Sharing a "Makhorka"

Perhaps it was a "guy thing." However, Yossale and Itchale did not see each other the next day and not the following.

Sharing stories created intimacy that felt uncomfortable. Or who knows? They were too tired of reminiscing day after day.

Only on the third evening, Yossale showed up at Itchale's barrack. Itchale offered the only chair they had to Yossale, while he sat on his mattress. It was the only time Yossale was taller than Itchale. They laughed, remembering how they used to compare their heights and other protruding organs—noses, for instance, when they were growing up.

Itchale did not realize how starved he was to vent his experiences since he had left home but particularly since his abduction.

Yossale did not have such a pressing need, perhaps because his life experiences were less dramatic than Itchale's. Years of living in the gulag, surrounded by people he had not learned to trust, taught him to keep his stories to himself. As the years passed, he felt like a smothered candle—out of vitality. He lost his curiosity about others until he met Itchale.

Itchale's presence reawakened his interest in others. Was it because of his old interest in Adel? It did not matter. His stories re-engaged him to life as though he lived vicariously through Itchale's experiences, including his love story. And he was grateful because he did not remember Itchale as a big talker. But Itchale, who was only a few days in the gulag, was still confused and bewildered. Yossale's eagerness to listen encouraged him to vent. He needed a listening ear. And he could trust his old friend. They did not need any introductions. They could continue where they had left off.

"So what happened on the train?" asked Yossale.

"Well, on the first day, when we were still in the Lvov area, we did not get any food or drink. The train was at the station for the rest of that day and the whole night. It was so cold that nobody could sleep. The crying and screaming of children and adults echoed in my ears for days. At daylight, the train took off. We were not told why we were waiting and where we were being taken. Through the wooden slits of the wagon, I could see we passed forests and traveled over bridges. We went through snow-covered fields and villages. By the alternating darkness and daylight, I figured that seven days had passed since the day we'd been abducted. When the train stopped, I had no idea where we were. At the first stop, we were allowed to get off and walk around. Those who had money bought some food; others stretched their limbs. I got off but stayed close to the train."

"Why didn't you run? Couldn't you try to escape?"

"We were surrounded by armed soldiers. So how far could I have run before I got a bullet in my back? And even if I could run, where was I supposed to run to? To the wilderness? There was nowhere to run. We waited to see where we were transported to." Itchale was a bit annoyed by the question. "Don't you think I would have done everything to go back to Adel? If it was only possible."

"Don't be upset, Itchale. I am sorry. What do I know? I didn't try to escape from the policeman either. And there was only one policeman with me. Not many armed soldiers. So go on." Yossale tried to appease his friend.

"When I got off the train, I managed to exchange some rags for a loaf of bread and an apple. Suddenly, without any warning, the train started moving. It continued doing just that for the rest of the journey. I jumped on, but many did not make it on time. The screaming and crying indicated that families were separated. Probably for good. There was nothing we could do but watch. The hunger, the thirst, and the freezing cold killed many in the wagons. Almost at every stop, frozen corpses were thrown off the train and left on the sidetracks. Most of them were children. It was horrible. By the end of our journey, there wasn't even one child left alive.

"I will never forget the mothers' wailing." Itchale sighed. He wiped his forehead, covering his eyes for a minute.

He pulled out a "makhorka" and offered one to Yossale. They lit up the cheap cigarettes, inhaling the smoke deep into their lungs.

The two men cemented their bond in silence.

Itchale was the first to break the silence. "After a while, you lose track of time. You don't know if it's day or night. Only the unexpected stops of the train kept me alert. On every stop, the soldiers took away some men. We never saw them again."

"They were probably taken away to prisons, to gulags, like ours. Who knows? They do with us whatever they want to," said Yossale in a somber voice. "I heard people are sent to such remote places as the Arctic Circle. And the conditions there are even more torturous than ours."

"And I heard we have to undergo reeducation in the communist doctrine. Is it true?" asked Itchale.

"Yes. I call it 'the yeshiva' (school of religious studies but also 'sitting' in Hebrew). We didn't want to attend the yeshiva at home—now, our parents got their wish—we are 'sitting' (imprisoned) here."

They laughed.

"You'll get used to it. Just agree with everything they say, and you'll survive." Yossale taught the newcomer the introduction to survival in the gulag.

Itchale nodded. What choice did he have?

"So what happened on the train?" asked Yossale.

"Every stop of the train raised our anxiety," he continued. "I wondered when and where would be 'my stop.' One day the train stopped and my 'lucky' number was called: 'Thirteen, walk over to the transporter on your left!'

"A coachman with a horse and an open carriage was waiting there impatiently. I was not alone. Twelve men were 'encouraged' by the soldiers, with well-aimed kicks and a few 'creative' curses that alluded to our maternal relatives, to get on to the waiting carriage. We took off with the coachman's 'blessing' to the mothers who brought these soldiers to the world. And not to exclude us—'the enemies of the people'—he scattered us with a hefty spitting."

"Where did he take you?"

"I was too cold and hungry to pay close attention to the road. We drove for a while deep into the woods. The country road was slippery. All I heard was the whistle of the arctic wind, the cursing and spitting of the coachman. His spittle froze in midair. When it felt as if we would never come to a stop, we arrived at a wooden gate of a camp. We knew, by now, that we were in Siberia, but where exactly, we did not know.

"Since I was the only one who spoke Russian, I asked the coachman, 'Where were we?'

"You are in a gulag in the Ural Mountains area," he said. "This is a logging camp. Here you will chop trees to help our effort in rebuilding what was damaged by our enemies," he added angrily.

"I guess that was our first 'reeducation' speech." Itchale smiled.

"But, as I told you," said Yossale, "not the last."

"Although I have no experience in logging, it sounded better than working in the coal mines."

"Here, at least, you are above ground," said Yossale. "Although I am not sure if it's truly better than underground."

Since he had first seen Itchale, he had felt he might still have hope to survive in the gulag. Otherwise, he thought, he might have killed himself. He knew he shouldn't say a word about it. Not at this point anyway.

"Do you know where exactly this gulag is located?" asked Itchale.

"Somewhere between the Ural Mountains and the cities of Omsk and Novosibirsk. But I heard the distance between these regions is over fifteen hundred kilometers."

"Incredible, I admit," said Itchale. "I was shocked when I arrived. I am still quite overwhelmed."

"At once, you are a no man. We and the guards belong to different species," Yossale echoed Itchale's words, nodding his head emphatically. He knew the feeling. Years in the gulag only deepened that sense of detachment from people and surroundings.

"However, when I got a mattress," continued Itchale, "the uniform with a serial number printed on the back of my shirt, and the heavy boots two sizes bigger than my feet, I knew that I 'had arrived' at a final destination. Here—I'll either survive or perish."

"You are a quick learner, Itchale. There is no 'thriving' here, only barely 'surviving' and death. Believe me, I think about death more than I think about surviving."

"Yossale, what are you talking about? We have to survive to go back home!"

"Home?" Yossale said it in almost a whisper.

*Itchale is new in this hell. He can still hope. Perhaps it's better for him if I give him some reality lessons.* Yossale did not share those thoughts with his friend.

"I knew a few who tried to escape—they were shot by the guards on the spot. Those have no mercy. Look at them. They are like hungry dogs, thirsty for their daily quota of blood. I guess they are rewarded for shooting a prisoner," said Yossale.

Itchale looked gloomy. "Where can you go even if you manage to escape? One look at the dark forest around us, the howling of the wolves and other wild life, makes you appreciate the opportunity to die by a man-made bullet."

"Or starvation," added Yossale. "And don't forget a well-aimed kick that folds you in half. Don't worry, in a short while you will look just like me—a toothless skeleton."

They laughed, their bodies leaning toward each other. For a brief moment, they were back in the shtetl, mischievous boys conspiring to do something naughty. They could complete each other's sentences.

Their friendship was restored, no doubt.

The camp was nestled within a dense Siberian forest and surrounded by a tall wooden fence in bad shape, rusty barbed wire, but with no watchtowers. Only several armed soldiers were patrolling inside the camp. By the looks of the soldiers, they had seen better days. Inside, there were two rows of dilapidated barracks in the middle of a rectangular yard.

"When I was assigned to my barrack, there were at least twenty men inside already. Each of the new arrivals was given a straw mattress, a filthy, thin blanket, and three hundred grams of bread. I found a corner near a window and rolled me a makhorka to smoke."

"You know that you can buy makhorkas at the camp. We have a small shop here, a laundry room, and there are even a few families with children. You see, Itchale, we could have had fun here, if we were only allowed to live."

"Don't give up yet, my friend. We are young and even you have something to look forward to!"

"To what exactly?" Yossale was smiling.

"To get a new set of teeth!" Itchale laughed, but Yossale was only slightly amused. He expected a funny answer but not that one. Itchale had touched a raw nerve.

Yossale thought he had nothing to look forward to. No wife nor family, and now—no teeth. He envied Itchale for his beautiful white teeth and muscular body. *I look like an old and decrepit man compared to him. We are the same age, for heaven's sake! His back is straight. Mine is bent like my broken spirit, and I did not lose a wife. Adel! He left her! Not fair. But he told me what happened. Poor man. Poor woman! Where is she now?*

Itchale watched his friend sinking into silence. He suspected that Yossale's sudden mood shift had to do with his laughter rather than with his last comment. But even if his life depended on it, he could not bring himself to ask Yossale, "How do you feel?"

*Men don't say things like that. He would be embarrassed. Better not to talk. He'll get over it.*

Yossale glanced at Itchale. *He knows me so well. I hope he does not say a word.* The old-new friends let silence fill the space between them.

The silence thickened, and the longer it lasted the more it challenged their renewed trust in each other.

Trust remains fragile even between old friends.

It was late. A new day of tree chopping was waiting for them in the morning. With great relief, they departed for the night, in silence still.

Their friendship shaken but unharmed.

# 27
## Adjustment to Hell

E very day of chopping and logging trees seemed to never end. Chopping trees for the Trans-Siberian railroad, or for the building of Soviet cities, was all they did.

The air of the very first morning in the gulag was crisp and cold. Each inmate-laborer was assigned to a specific area in the woods. Each was given a pair of gloves, an axe, and a chainsaw.

The equipment came with a loud warning though. "If any of you scums of the earth dare to raise an axe on anything but a tree—the next thing you will all see is your head chopped off." Armed guards watched them constantly.

Breaks were not permitted. Every laborer had a daily quota of trees to complete. After a few times of hitting the tree at a wrong angle, Itchale learned how to use the axe correctly. He worked fast in spite of the blisters that grew on his hands even with the gloves. His gloves were worn-out. Used by generations of inmates. *They were probably stripped off a corpse*, thought Itchale while rubbing his swollen palms.

Although the hungry inmates waited for the lunchtime break, they were startled by the shrieking sound of the siren tearing the silence of the woods and their eardrums alike.

The exhausted men lined up to receive a tin cup with hot tea and a bowl of an additional unidentified liquid called "soup." The difference between the two types of liquid was in the strange objects that floated in one. In that of the soup, there were a few tired vegetables and sad noodles floating around. Each laborer also received dark and soggy bread. The entire meal looked like the sour face of the person (man or woman) who distributed it and smelled like stale sweat. Who could tell the difference after twelve hours of chopping wood?

Once Itchale got to know his surroundings and estimated his chances of survival there, he quickly overcame his initial shock and got to work, literally and figuratively. When he arrived at the gulag, he did not know any of the men. However, he quickly befriended some. It was a matter of survival. Not all were Jewish. He learned that at least a third of the men were convicted criminals. He kept a distance from them. Others were political prisoners. He had to be careful with those as well. One could not tell who was an NKVD informant. The minority were like him—abducted from the streets and imprisoned without any formal accusation.

There were several families with children who lived in the camp in separate quarters. Watching the women with children at the camp, Itchale was glad Adel had been spared that kind of suffering. At the time, he did not know that women whose husbands were sent to gulags were victimized as well. They heard from new prisoners that friends and neighbors often turned against those women, sometimes for fear of associating with "wives of enemies of the people." In the gulag, contact with the outside world was forbidden. They got their news only from the new inmates.

Itchale, or "Izak" as he was soon called in the camp, immersed himself in the routine of life in the camp. They woke up when it was still dark outside, when God was still asleep. And worked from dawn to dusk. Everybody had to work. Even the sick could not get a day off. Breakfast was a slice of soggy bread. Only on very cold days would they get a cup of hot fluid. After breakfast, they were immediately escorted by guards to work. On the march to the woods, they were daily threatened to be shot if they took even one step out of line. They cut and chopped wood, day after day; that's all they did.

Much of the inmates' existence in the gulag was dictated by hunger. They received food only according to their productivity. Seven hundred grams of bread, the maximum amount allowed, was for a laborer only.

Keeping them half-starved, cold, and terrorized by violent inmates and by soldiers was one way to keep them under control.

Inside the barracks, it was either too hot and humid or very cold. Most men, who were too exhausted to wash themselves, were infested with lice and their mattresses with bedbugs. Even Itchale, who tried to keep clean, suffered.

The floor was usually covered with slippery mud. And the whole barrack was dimly lit by only one small light bulb.

The constant hunger, the fatigue, the filth, the lice, the long days and short nights, or the long white nights—all bred despair.

Itchale asked himself many times, *What keeps me going? What for?* Most of the time he answered himself. *I hope to see Adel and the rest of my family again.*

One evening, Itchale discussed with Yossale hope and "the meaning of life in the gulag."

Yossale said, "Had I not met you here, I don't know if I could have survived another week."

That statement did not fall on deaf ears. It deserved another day of silent contemplation by both men.

The next time they met, Yossale asked, "Do you think about Adel?"

Itchale wondered if it wasn't Yossale who thought about Adel.

"Do you think she is faithful to you?" *He is crossing a line,* thought Itchale.

"No doubt," he replied. "If I had been a knight during the crusades, I could have left her without a chastity belt on."

They laughed.

After these conversations, Itchale wondered, *What fantasies does his shrunken brain have about my wife?*

Years later, still in the gulag, the two men were still close friends, holding each other's life in the palm of their hands.

Yossale dared to ask once again, "Itchale, are you still thinking of Adel?"

"I do," answered Itchale. "And you? Are you still thinking of my wife?"

During the years they spent in the gulag, it was humor that kept and maintained their humanity. It was their sense of humor that enabled them to keep their reality in perspective and their laughter that helped them feel normal. Humor was the oxygen for their hopes.

"When I arrived at the gulag, I thought about her all the time," said Itchale. "I used to ask new prisoners who arrived from the Lvov area if they had seen her. After a while, I stopped asking. I am afraid she died. Truly, I cannot imagine her surviving the war on her own. Without documents, work, or speaking the language. She is Adel—too gentle and too young."

"Ah, what do you know? She might be tougher than you think. She is probably alive somewhere," said Yossale.

"I hope you are right."

Was it a statement of faith or doubt? Time would tell.

# 28
## Making a Life

After a separation of almost five years, Adel and Itchale were finally reunited. They rejoiced in each other quietly that night.

He could not stop asking, "Can you believe it?" and "How—?"

And she could not stop laughing and crying at the same time. If she only had any strength left in her, she would have swirled around him dancing. But although exhilarated, she was also exhausted. So she sat on his mattress, their bed, and did not take her eyes off him. She felt if she looked aside even for one moment, he would disappear, like a dream she might wake from.

She longed to touch him. "Come, Itchale, sit next to me." He was skinny, but his body was warm. She could feel his muscles. She put her head on his chest against his heart. His heart beat was reassuring. Her excitement took its toll, and she closed her eyes. She opened them for a minute. She was still in his lap.

He was stroking her hair.

"Look at that beauty. Pure gold," he mumbled.

*Pure gold. She looks like an angel*, he thought.

He leaned over and kissed her forehead lightly so as not to wake her, and very gently, he put her sleepy body closer to the wall and lay down along her side in a spooning position. Just the way they used to sleep in their previous life, in Lvov.

There was not much privacy in a barrack with dozens of ears listening. The routine of the gulag could not be interrupted only because a woman had found her way into the gulag and back to her man.

The morning came too soon. He did not want to get up. She could not. Her body was aching for rest after years of moving from place to place. But they had to. Itchale had to go back to work, and Adel had to register with the camp's authorities. They looked at each other, still in disbelief, and smiled.

She was the first one to talk. "It's going to be good. You'll see."

Itchale gave her a peck on her cheek. He did not talk before he had his first cigarette.

*Unbelievable. She did not lose her optimism*, he thought.

He lit up a makhorka, inhaled the smoke, and exhaled it slowly.

The siren tore their eardrums and their intimacy. It was a brutal reminder of the reality awaiting them outside.

It was time to say goodbye until the evening.

*Please God, only until the evening, she begged in her heart. Please let him come back to me safe.*

Before they parted, Itchale asked Adel if she remembered Yossale, their childhood friend from the shtetl.

"Yes, I remember. Is he here? I want to see him!" she exclaimed.

"You will meet him. He has been here years. We see each other almost every day."

"How is he?"

"That's the reason I'm telling you about him now. You may not recognize him. I want to prepare you. He has aged a lot. He also lost all his teeth, poor man."

"Is he sick, God forbid?"

"He is not healthy. But who is? Don't worry. He lost only his teeth but not his sense of humor."

"I always liked him," she said.

"Well, he liked you too. He still does. He hasn't changed. Me neither. I still like you."

They laughed.

She leaned over and kissed him briefly on the lips. This was the reassurance he needed for the day. They embraced in a quick hug and left the barrack.

A new chapter in their life had started.

Adel was assigned a job—to work with children in a kindergarten of sort. She was told that for her work she would receive three hundred grams of bread and soup. *Life is good*, she thought.

She was supposed to start her job the next day. Meanwhile, she went back to the barrack and started cleaning. Cleaning was her "safe haven." It kept her sanity. She loved vigorous work. It grounded her.

"It makes me feel alive," she used to say to those who wondered about her energy surges. Recalling her frantic cleaning of their basement apartment in Lvov the day after Itchale disappeared, she said to herself. *And it keeps frightening thoughts away.*

Night after night, the couple sat on their mattress, separated from the rest of the men who lived in that barrack by a blanket.

They stayed inside when it was cold, outside when the weather permitted, and exchanged stories. Adel and Itchale told each other of their whereabouts from the day Itchale left their apartment in Lvov with a heavy heart and Adel went looking for him. Each talked in turn. Sometimes, they completed each other's sentences—their stories intertwined. Yossale would join them sometimes but not too often. Although welcomed by Adel (He still loved her; she felt his yearning and so did Itchale.), he did not feel comfortable interrupting the couple's intimacy. He surprised them once, shortly after he heard from Itchale that Adel was in the camp. As he walked into the barrack, he could smell their intimacy. He ran away as if bitten by a snake before they noticed him.

The others in the barrack eavesdropped. Nobody dared to interfere.

Itchale lit up a makhorka. He glimpsed at Adel.

*Does she really want to hear my story in the gulag?*

She assured him she did. She would rather listen to him talking than to have to relive her nightmares when telling him her story. She was not ready to tell it all yet.

He inhaled the smoke and exhaled it, puffing out rings of smoke.

*Just like he was twelve years old*, she thought. She smiled at him. He looked at her in one of his long green glances (to die for that look, she thought), and in a quiet voice told his wife about the incredible day when he saw a mirage walking toward him from the woods.

"The day you found me, I stopped chopping wood for a moment to roll me a makhorka. While inhaling the smoke, I looked up. To my amazement, I saw a woman's figure walking toward me. Where had she come from? Had the hunger and fatigue caused me to hallucinate? Was it a mirage? I closed my eyes and opened them again. Can anyone else see her? I was alone. The others were somewhere in the forest. It was a skeleton in a woman's figure. The skeleton was walking toward the gulag! Was she lost in the taiga? She looked like an old woman. Sinking into the deep snow and then rising again to take another labored step. As she got closer, I could see she was wearing a babushka's head kerchief, a man's coat over a patched dress, and rags wrapped around her feet. And when she was really close, I noticed a blonde lock peeking from underneath her head kerchief."

Adel smiled. That rebellious lock gave me away.

"The blonde skeleton was not an old woman. Just a very skinny young woman. And that blonde lock—looked so familiar. How was that possible?

"You were alive! You survived the war! You were here! How did you find me? There was no doubt. It was you! My Adel."

Itchale touched his mustache, a smile in his eyes. They were shining suspiciously. She moved closer and touched his arm.

Go on, she "nudging" him with her eyes.

While Itchale talked, Adel's mind wandered, summarizing her life of the last years. Almost five years and close to twenty thousand kilometers, crisscrossing, mostly by foot, the two continents: parts of Europe and Asian Russia. From Lvov in the Ukraine through Siberia and Mongolia to Vladivostok in the Far East and all the way back, through Kazakhstan and back to Siberia. Somewhere in a gulag, north of Novosibirsk and south of Omsk, she found her man. *Itchale. My bashert, the love of my life. My husband! It is him! Next to me! Pinch me; I am not dreaming!*

"Itchale, did you miss me?"

"I don't miss those who are in my heart."

She is surprised by his response, but she is also touched.

"Did you miss me?" he asked.

"I did. Although you are in my heart, I missed your physical presence."

*She always had the winning last word*, he thought.

The two lovers exchanged a smile. Adel lifted Itchale's hand to her lips and kissed it softly. His heart skipped a beat. His body recalled her touch. He left his arm on her lap.

"Did you kiss me when we met?"

"Did I kiss you? Have you forgotten already? I gave you a peck on your lips for sure."

"Does that count?" Itchale teased her.

"But you held me so tight I felt my ribs cracking," she said, laughing.

"I had to hold you," he replied. "You looked like you were about to faint."

"Well, I was hungry."

"For me?"

"For you too, my dear, and for bread." She laughed.

"You looked like a starved skeleton. Do you remember? I left you standing there and ran to the barrack to get you the whole portion of bread I received for the day. I handed you the bread and meanwhile rolled a makhorka. By the time I finished rolling the makhorka—you had inhaled the whole bread!"

"True," she said. "I was starved."

She was unapologetic but, nevertheless, embarrassed by his description of her hunger-driven, non-civil behavior.

"Then you took me to the barrack. I was shocked to see how you men lived. A pigsty was cleaner than this barrack. And your bed? Oy vey to that bed. A filthy straw mattress laid on the concrete floor. And the blanket? There were more holes in the blanket than *blanket*."

Itchale watched her in silence. *What can I say? She's right. How will I protect her when she realizes where we truly are?*

As if reading his mind, she said, "This is a labor camp, like a jail. I understand. Don't worry about me, Itchale. I'll manage. You'll see. It will be easier together. Do you remember? On the second day, I got to work. I scrubbed the concrete floor, the filthy windows, and the wooden walls. Then, I put a couple of men to chop some ice and heat it in a big boiler. I could imagine the lice and bedbugs that crawled all over the barrack." She shuddered in disgust. "I pulled off all the blankets from the mattresses and put them into the boiling water. There was no soap, so I threw in a bunch of dry grass and with a big stick stirred it until it was clean. When it was all clean, I hung it to dry in the cold wind. When it was dry, it was crisp and fragrant." Adel took a deep breath, as if she could smell the Siberian dry grass.

"You then took a blanket and hung it as a barrier around our mattress, our bed now, to create privacy. You said, 'We are a couple after all.'"

They smiled in delight. They loved each other's detailed storytelling.

"I don't understand how you commanded those men, the 'walking dead,' to help you clean the barrack? You managed to do what the armed guards could not!"

"I told you not to worry about me. I manage.

Did you ever doubt my faithfulness?" She surprised him with her direct question.

She noticed he did not answer right away.

*Is there a catch there? What does she expect me to say?* he thought.

"Would you like me to ask you?" he responded.

"Well, if you have to ask me, then—" she let the rest of the sentence hang in the air.

He put his arm around her. She breathed in relief. "I know you never doubted me," she told him.

He squeezed her shoulder lightly in response.

*He asks what he wants to hear*, she thought. She shrugged. *We have a lifetime ahead of us to tell each other whatever we went through. And there will still be things we will never ask about.*

Besides, she believed, that extreme pain, like great joy, had no words.

Adel adjusted fast to life in the gulag.

One night, a couple of months later, she approached her husband carefully.

She had a plan he might not approve.

"Itchale tayere (dear)," she said. "I have noticed there are very few guards and no watchtowers. The guards are armed but hungry and tired like you, the laborers they are in charge of. I have seen the surrounding fence. It is broken in a few places. This is how I got in. And if I got in, I can get out."

"That is your plan? To get out through the broken fence?" Itchale raised his voice.

"Sha, sha, people may hear you. What did I say?"

Too late.

"Don't even think about it, Adel!" he said sharply. "It's too dangerous. The guards do not hesitate to shoot or beat an inmate to death. And you are now an inmate like the rest of us!"

She was not going to give up on her plan, but she would keep it to herself, until next time. Meanwhile, she would confront him with facts.

"We'll see," she told him. "If I ever leave the camp, I promise to be careful."

Itchale was worried. *Will she get us into trouble?* He was not convinced she would keep her promise. He knew her "determination"—the way she calls it—or her "stubbornness," the way he sees it.

From the moment she brought up her plan to escape from the gulag, it became her secret. The first secret she kept from him. They were both careful not to talk about it. The fear to discuss such a plan drew a wedge between them. Adel had to do something.

*I am not going to stay in a prison and neither will my husband*, she said to herself. *But first, I have to get stronger and take care of Itchale.*

*He is too thin. He does not tolerate hunger as well as I do. And I am worried about his cough. I must do something before it is too late.*

She kept those thoughts to herself but continued planning a way out.

It was 1945 already. There were rumors the Germans were being defeated by the Russian army and the war was about to be over. They heard the gulag was going to be relocated deeper into the Urals or to the Arctic Circle. Military trucks came night after night and transported laborers and guards to the new locations. The presence of the guards became scarce and such was the distribution of food. People were scared of the unknown.

Something was about to happen. *It is time to leave before we are on the next transport, God forbid*, she thought.

One morning, she did not go to work. Nobody checked anymore. Without telling Itchale—he would have stopped her—she decided to go to a nearby village to sell whatever she had in the basket she brought with her and buy whatever she could get to supplement their food.

Because she came in to the gulag by foot, she knew which direction to go and how far the closest village was. It was only a couple of hours away. She watched the guards for a while to see when they changed shifts. That was the best time to slip out. She marked in advance a crack in the fence, so she could identify it when she got out and when she came back in. She took the two colorful dresses she received in Kazakhstan from her landlady some time ago in exchange for her slip. She cut them into pieces, put on her Baba Yaga attire, and slipped out through the marked crack.

Without any difficulty, she retraced her steps to the nearby village. A two-hour walk was easy like a breeze.

Although she did not miss the walking, she enjoyed being a free person, not fenced in. She had no difficulty selling her colorful rags in the local market.

Adel walked out of the gulag with a light basket and a heavy heart. She returned with lightness in her heart but with a heavy basket.

When she arrived at the gulag later that day, it was almost dark and Itchale was upset and worried. But when she invited him, Yossale, and the other men in the barrack to a royal meal she prepared from the eggs, milk, and bread she brought from the village, he was proud to be "the king of the hour"—Adel's husband. He was clearly bathing in the envious looks of the other men.

Unfortunately, she could not do it too often. It was too dangerous, and she had nothing left to sell.

As time went by, she got stronger. Itchale was feeling better and his cough had almost disappeared. Adel brought up her plan again. She tried to convince her husband that now was the right time to escape from the gulag.

"Look, I came into the gulag through the broken fence and walked out a few times. Nobody saw me, and if they saw, they did not care. The camp is in chaos. This is the time to take our chance and run! Let's go!"

He hesitated.

"Are you afraid to leave?" She teased him with a truth he did not care to hear.

"Let's go? I think you have lost your mind. Go where? If it was possible to go, don't you think I would have gone a long time ago?" Itchale was clearly upset.

Adel did not like confrontations, but she did not shy away from them either.

"Didn't I walk in and out of the gulag a few times? Didn't I find my way across the land? You need to trust me! What is the worst that can happen to us?" she asked defiantly. "We will either die here or in another gulag we will be transported to. We will die from starvation for sure. If we run, in the worst case, the guards will shoot us or the bears and wolves will feast on us. Of all options, I prefer the bears."

Itchale did not interrupt Adel's monologue. He listened carefully and came to the same conclusion: *Why wait to die in the gulag? Perhaps there is a chance of survival outside? She made it after all.*

He was finally convinced.

"Itchale, how long have I been in the gulag?"

"Almost a year," he answered.

*She was never good with numbers,* he thought. "You arrived around the beginning of spring 1944 and, if I'm not mistaken, we are at the beginning of winter 1945."

She could not remember how long exactly.

How could he expect her to remember? She was half dead when she arrived at the gulag. Starved and weak. The days in the gulag were marked by the siren for work, for the distribution of food, and by personal events. Being cut off from the external world, prisoners perceived time subjectively—depending on their interpretation of events or rumors. Subjective perception of time differs from the objective-chronological measure of time. For Adel, twenty thousand kilometers were measured only by the time it took her to find Itchale.

She perceived a year in the gulag as too long to stay in a prison and too short to be with her husband.

# ESCAPE FROM
# THE GULAG

# 29
# Two Graves in the Snow

"Let's go! But where to? Do you know which way to go? By foot? By train?" Itchale asked.

"Itchale, Itchale, my heart brought me here, and my heart will lead us out in the right direction," she responded.

*Can I trust her heart as a compass? It sounds ridiculous. On the other hand, the whole idea of escape is crazy.*

But once the idea of escape was introduced to him, the possibility of staying in the gulag was no option any longer.

Itchale and Adel shared their plan with Yossale and invited him to join them. Yossale refused.

"I have no strength left in me to go. I'm afraid to hold you back. But if you make it back to Izbica, say 'hello' to my family—if any of them is still alive." These were his last words.

They never saw or heard from Yossale again. He probably died in the gulag.

At that time, rumors spread about ghettos and death camps the Nazis had built and the demise of millions of Jews from all over Europe, but especially from Poland. There was even one rumor about the first and probably worst ghetto built in Poland. That was the Izbica ghetto. They did not know that in Lvov, the city they escaped to from Poland, a ghetto was built in 1941, the same year of the Izbica ghetto and a year after Itchale was abducted and Adel started her search for him.

Itchale and Adel wanted to go home to Izbica. They needed to see if any of their family was alive.

They quietly packed a basket and, at dawn, slipped out of the barrack and through the board Adel had marked earlier—they left the gulag forever.

Even if a guard noticed, he would not bother to shoot them. Why should he waste ammunition on two skeletons doomed to die by starvation or by wild animals anyway? What chance did they have to survive the Siberian wilderness?

She walked fast. He was behind.

*Is he guarding me?* she wondered. *Or is he still hesitant about leaving?*

Adel slowed down, closing the gap between them. She watched him with some concern.

*He left the gulag after years of being imprisoned,* she thought. *Will the gulag ever leave him? What if he has forgotten what it means to be free, to find work and food when it's not handed to him,* she wondered. *I will not take my eyes off him,* she promised herself.

As it turned out—she underestimated him.

Itchale promised himself the same. He lagged behind because she knew the way, and he was "keeping her back"— guarding her.

He was worried about her health. He noticed how thin and pale she was. She even threw up a few times.

"You have nothing to worry about," she assured him. "It is probably just a stomach flu."

*She has suffered enough*, he thought. *Now it is my turn to take care of her.*

He had no doubt he was capable of doing whatever it took to survive. *If my gentle Adel did it—walking for years, sleeping in the open fields, eating whatever she could find, working at whatever was available, and chasing trains—I can do it too*, was his conviction.

He straightened his back and raised his chin. He felt free. Only his body was imprisoned. She imbued him with hope and courage he forgot he once had. All he wanted to do was protect her, erase her pain, make her laugh and sing again.

They were walking along the Trans-Siberian train tracks. Adel was not feeling well. She threw up, especially in the mornings, and was nauseated for hours. Dizzy and getting weaker, she needed to get help.

"That is not a good sign," she said. "I cannot afford to get sick." She felt helpless. *How will I take care of him if I am sick?*

Itchale urged her to leave their path along the train tracks and walk into the dense woods to look for a village. Many small villages hid in the woods and could not be seen from the tracks. She was too weak to argue.

Suddenly she went limp.

"Adel! Wake up!"

He took a handful of snow and rubbed her face. She opened her eyes.

"Thank goodness, you are alive!" He lifted her and pressed her to his chest. He rubbed her arms to warm her up. She was so fragile. He was scared. He was not going to lose her!

"Adel, stay with me. Stay awake. We will get to a village soon." Adel heard his words as if said from a distance. She felt a wave of heat coming over her as she passed out.

When she woke up, she was lying on a bench inside a cottage, and two worried faces were looking at her. One was Itchale's. The other was a strange woman. Adel sat up.

"What happened to me?"

"You fainted, and I carried you to the village. We were very close to this woman's cottage. But because it was hidden so well, we could not see it."

"You carried me on your back?"

"How else could I have carried you? You think you are light? You are skin and bones but heavy," he said half-jokingly.

"Or perhaps you are not as strong as you used to be," she replied.

*Her sharp tongue is back*, he thought. *If she can say that, then she is fine. She is out of danger.*

"I am Yanna." The woman took a damp towel and wiped Adel's face. She checked Adel's pulse.

"She'll be fine. Your wife?"

Itchale nodded.

He was sitting next to Adel, both facing Yanna like two pupils in front of a teacher.

The woman looked at them, smiling.

"You," she said to Adel, "are pregnant, not sick."

"Pregnant?! Did I hear right? I am pregnant. Forgive me, but how do you know?"

*Is she a witch?* Adel felt like throwing up in panic. *All we need is my pregnancy!*

"Itchale, what are we going to do?"

Itchale was shocked to hear Yanna's diagnosis. He too questioned her. "How can you tell?"

"Young man, I have been a midwife since before the two of you were born. This is your first pregnancy, isn't it?"

Itchale scratched his head. "What should we do now?" he asked both women.

Adel answered, "We go on. Now that I know it's not an illness."

Yanna listened to them. She turned to Itchale. "This is her first pregnancy. If you want to keep it, your wife will need to eat well and rest. You should not go to wherever you planned on going. Especially not in this weather."

"Where can we stay?" Adel asked, the expected practical question.

"Here. With me. I will help you, and your husband will help me with my chores."

"This is a miracle," said Adel.

Itchale did not believe in miracles, only in *coincidences*. And all coincidences, in his opinion, were explainable.

"How do you explain the woman's offer then? If not a miracle?" she asked.

"A coincidence of menschlichkeit," he said triumphantly.

She laughed. He did not know that this was how she explained all man-made miracles.

Adel cleaned Yanna's cottage and cooked. And Itchale chopped wood and did all other maintenance work needed. Yanna was a war widow with no children. Those two, who showed up on her doorstep, were the "miracle" she had prayed for.

About seven months later, Adel gave birth to a little girl. They named her Bela after Adel's mother. The older woman taught the young parents how to bathe the baby and how to feed her. She was their mother and grandmother. They were grateful. Thanks to her, they learned to enjoy their first parenthood. The chubby baby girl looked like a cherub, with her blonde hair and her big blue eyes. She looked healthy and happy.

When the baby was a few weeks old, the little family said goodbye to the woman they called "Mama." The mom who had saved their lives.

They walked with the baby for days, sleeping in villages and along the train tracks. Sometimes, they snuck onto a train. Sometimes, they were kicked away by peasants. Hunger never let them forget its presence.

"Itchale, the child is sick. I don't like that cough," said Adel one day. Bela was crying and coughing, coughing and crying. Because of hunger and weakness, Adel could not nurse the baby. Her milk had dried up. They were far from a village and there was no train on the horizon. The terrified parents took turns in holding the baby, trying to comfort her. But to no avail. Little Bela slipped away. She was about ten months old when she closed her beautiful eyes forever.

Adel cried silently, as she always did. Itchale could not even hold them—not his grieving wife nor his baby daughter, his firstborn.

He walked away and started digging in the snow, a little grave. She joined him. With their bare hands, they dug a grave in the ice-covered ground for their baby. The earth opened its frozen womb to receive the little girl.

The parents marked the grave with a small rock. They stood there for a while, frozen in disbelief.

When they walked away, their hearts were vacant and their tears dry. They could not look back.

They walked in silence. Both knew that unbearable pain, just like great joy, has no words.

Joy evaporated from their lives with Bela's death.

Instead came unbearable pain.

They walked through Siberia, listless, heading south.

They were in Siberia, living and working in one of the villages temporarily. They had to get stronger and save some money to continue their journey, when they found out Adel was pregnant again.

"Life is stronger than death, after all," she said.

"It was an accident," said Itchale.

Accident or the force of life—she gave birth to a healthy baby boy.

They named him "Hersh" or "Hershale" after Adel's father. Hershale looked just like Itchale, his father: dark hair, olive skin, and green eyes. He was a smart baby. A delightful little person. Hershale was walking already and saying his first words when, like his sister, he became ill. He got pneumonia.

They lived at that time in a tribal village. The desperate parents' cries summoned to their hut the local shaman. He was the tribe's healer of all ailments. The parents were skeptical about the shaman's ability to help, but what choice did they have?

The despondent parents watched the shaman's ritual and prayer and helplessly saw how life was leaving their child's body.

That was the first time Adel heard Itchale's sobbing. He was lamenting while digging again a hole in the ground with his bare hands.

Adel did not let go, pressing her child's still warm little body to her chest. Kissing his forehead, his delicate face, his rosy lips, his chest, his tiny hands—each finger separately, his feet, and little toes—over and over again—to be etched on her mind and heart. Never to be forgotten.

"Maybe he'll wake up?" she cried, knowing the answer. It started raining.

*Will we ever stop crying?*

"Adel," she heard Itchale's voice. "It's time."

"Time for what?"

"To let go."

They returned Hershale too—to Mother Earth.

"Ashes to ashes—dust to dust—"

A week later, with hollow hearts and empty arms, they left the little grave and the village behind.

They embarked on a train that took them away from Siberia, the gulag, and the two little graves. They went south to Uzbekistan.

# 30
# Reigning in the "Kolkhoz"

"The Soviet government was about to let Polish Jewish people leave Russia and return to Poland."

That was the rumor they heard from a couple of Jewish wanderers they met during their escape from the gulag.

"The government was organizing transports from Tashkent in Uzbekistan." Another rumor. Itchale and Adel had no way of confirming the rumor. But what difference would it make anyway? They needed a direction. Now, they had one—southwest to Uzbekistan.

They finally made it to Uzbekistan. But the long journey, by foot and by trains, the pregnancies, the births of their babies, and above all, their deaths, took its toll. They had to stop some place, heal their bodies, and nourish their souls.

"Grief is not an illness we can expect to heal or recover from," she said to her husband. "But I can feel better. I can choose to give life a chance."

He listened. What could he tell her? She was the one who had carried two babies under her heart for months and then, after she saw them grow, had to bury them. What can you tell a mother? He felt helpless.

She had hoped he would eventually come to the same conclusion. She needed him to stay with her. *Right now, he is with me only in body*, she thought.

And his body recoiled from her touch.

"Itchale, I need you. You'll see—we'll have more children. We'll make a new life for ourselves in a free world. We are going home!"

And Itchale got better. She was a life force pulling him by his sleeve.

"Get better! Stay with me! I need you!"

Both needed to be needed by the other. It was a justification for their existence.

They heard it was easy to find work in a kolkhoz, a farm owned collectively by farmers who had to give away their privately-owned family farms to the government.

They were accepted to the kolkhoz with very few inquiries. No one was bothered by the fact they were Polish Jews or refugees. They adjusted fast and well to the agricultural life—living by nature's schedule and not by their own. They made friends with their Muslim neighbors. In fact, Itchale picked up some Arabic and could even read in the Quran.

Adel became a cook in the communal kitchen. She learned to prepare new dishes, and she loved it. It reminded her of her life in Mongolia and Kazakhstan.

"I feel at home," she would tell Itchale, smiling. He felt relieved when he saw with what ease she made friends. *She is not singing yet*, he thought. *That will come too, I hope.*

The kolkhoz sent Itchale to a driver's school.

"I graduated with honors when I reassembled a truck from scratch," he told his wife with pride.

He became a truck driver for the kolkhoz. With the truck, he delivered a variety of products throughout the continents.

He would disappear for days. Adel worried. The war was barely over, but there was still danger on those remote roads—drunk drivers, desperate robbers, or driver's fatigue. However, she never complained. She knew intuitively Itchale needed space after years in confinement, to grieve his way. Space, even from her.

Men, she believed, need more space to breathe than women. Needless to say, she perceived men as the weaker of the species, who nevertheless deserved her respect.

Itchale was regarded so highly he was offered a position as head of the kolkhoz. To Adel's dismay, he was ready to accept the offer.

"Are you out of your mind?" she raised her voice.

"Oy Itchale, is this your dream? To wear an Uzbek yarmulke? You didn't want to wear one at your parents' home—but theirs you like?"

Itchale laughed against his will.

*She's killing me*, he thought while laughing.

That was the first time she had heard him laugh since Hershale's death.

*Thank God for that*, she thought.

But she was still serious. "I want to remind you, we did not come to settle here. We are on our way home—to Izbica! We are not staying in Russia!"

He was impressed but not convinced yet.

So she pulled out her ultimate ammunition. "You will stay here only over my dead body."

He knew it was time to give in and leave the kolkhoz. He was not ready to see her dead body.

Life without her was no life at all.

# 31

## A Silent Journey

They had to go through the capital, Tashkent, in order to join the group of Jews leaving for Poland.

Tashkent reminded Adel of other cities she had passed through in Asian Russia. The mosques, the typical Asian faces, and their colorful outfits, even the smells were all familiar.

*I feel as if I have seen these places—Tashkent, Alma-Ata, Ulaanbaatar—in another lifetime*, she thought. *I was young then, scared, searching for Itchale. What did I know?* She sighed. She felt tired and empty. She had enough of running, of delivering life only to bury it shortly after. All she wanted was to go back home and rest.

They walked around the city, searching for familiar faces—Yiddish or Polish speaking people. They found a group ready to leave for Poland. All survivors of gulags and prisons. Each licking his own wounds. The Soviet government provided them with a truck and a driver to take them the forty-three hundred kilometers to the Polish border. They started their journey home. Each to his own home, or more accurately, what home used to be. They heard rumors of death camps, but no one knew for sure what had happened to their loved ones: if there would be a house; if the neighbors of yesterday would accept them willingly today. They needed to believe that somebody survived. The journey home was long and silent.

# BACK HOME
# TO POLAND

# 32
# A Big Void in the "Shtetl"

Izbica was once called "The Jewish Capital."
About five years earlier, when they had escaped to Russia,
there were about five thousand Jews and less than one thousand
Christians. But when they came back, there wasn't even a shadow
of a Jew left. The cemetery on the hill was full though. The shtetl
looked like hollow eyes—vacant of life.

Former neighbors, who were apprehensive to meet them,
insisted they did not know what had happened to their families.
They "did not see or hear anything." And of course, they all "hated
the Nazis."

Adel and Itchale were not welcomed, to say the least. The
town was shrouded in a cloud of fear and suspicion. Adel held
on to Itchale's arm. They did not leave each other's side, drawing
confidence and comfort from the other's closeness.

They walked in what used to be their shtetl and was now
just another typical Polish town but "clean" of Jews.

Overwhelmed by grief, they cried. "All dead! God in Heaven,
how did You allow that to happen?"

They walked in the streets as though passing through a
tunnel—no ground, no walls to hold on to. The once familiar
appeared strange now.

Itchale helped Adel climb the wooded hill overlooking the
town where the old Jewish cemetery used to be. As young lovers,

they used to hide there from curious eyes. Telling each other secrets, while their bodies touched occasionally in excitement. Now, to their horror, the cemetery hill was covered with new graves. Some had headstones. Most did not. Headstones were ripped off from old gravesites. They saw them later on sidewalks and walls. The Nazis and the locals used the Jewish headstones as building material.

The synagogue was inhabited by a family.

The Star of David and the sign in Hebrew were still attached.

*Is it irony? Ignorance? Or indifference?* they wondered when walking by.

The houses of Itchale's parents, of brothers and sisters, and Adel's father's house were destroyed beyond recognition.

Miraculously, Zelda's house closest to the riverbank was still intact and unlocked. Zelda's favorite dress lay on a chair, her shoes next to it. Her children's clothes folded in a drawer, ready to be worn. Her husband's jacket hanging in the hallway. It seemed as though Zelda's family had left briefly and were about to walk in any minute.

Although not empty, the house felt like a graveyard, while they themselves were the ghosts. Cobwebs in the corners. Ghosts trapped in the shadows.

"I don't want to touch anything," she said to Itchale while wiping off the dust from the kitchen table. There, where Itchale's small brown suitcase with her wedding dress in it once lay, in a different lifetime.

On their first night at Zelda's house, they heard a knock on the door. Itchale went to open it. One of Zelda's neighbors stood there with a basket.

"I have something to tell you. You may want to hear it." Itchale invited him in. He looked apprehensive but determined to talk to the young couple he had known since childhood. Adel recognized him immediately. She used to play with his children. They sat down in the kitchen.

The neighbor took out from his basket a jar of milk, a sausage, and a loaf of dark bread.

"You must be hungry. That's all I have. Eat."

Adel and Itchale thanked him. They swallowed their saliva. The smell of food was dizzying, but they did not touch the food. Not in front of him anyway. They wanted to hear what he had come to tell them.

"My wife and I loved your family. But we could not do anything when they were taken away by the Germans. I promised Zelda to take care of her house, and that we did." He looked down, his voice turning into a whisper. "Let me tell you what happened. Both of your families were among the first ones to be transported to the ghetto. We knew that Jews were brought into the ghetto from all over Europe, not just from Poland. Later we heard that your parents, Izak, escaped from the ghetto. But unfortunately, they were captured and shot. I don't know where they were buried. The rest of the Jews in town were sent from the ghetto to the death camps not far from here. The trains left from the Izbica train station, day and night, in one direction only. We all knew Jews were murdered in the ghetto and in the camps. Only a few, like you, came back to town after the war, but no one remained. Are you going to stay?" His quiet, steady tone gave them chills.

Unknownst to them, in 1941, shortly after Adel and Izak escaped to Russia, their families were sent by the Nazis first to the Izbica ghetto. From the ghetto, they were later deported to the death camps of Belzec, Sobibor, Majdanek, and others.

Most of them did not survive. Itchale's parents, Henia and Wolf, stayed in the ghetto from 1941 until 1943. In April 1943, they managed to escape from the ghetto to the villages of Orlow and Tarnogora, not far from Izbica. However, in July 1944, they were captured by a Nazi officer and shot in Izbica's town square. Henia was about forty-six years old, and Wolf about 51.

Adel got up from the table and walked away. They could hear her wailing.

*I fulfilled my promise to Zelda*, said the neighbor to himself. He took out a small packet of zloty and put it on the kitchen table. His question was still hanging in the air, unanswered. But by the look of the couple, he knew they were not going to stay in the house. He left the money. That was his offer to buy the house.

Itchale did not lift his eyes when the neighbor slipped out as fast as he could without saying goodbye.

The couple was left to cope with the news: Adel in the living room, Itchale in the kitchen. The bedroom remained empty that night.

At dawn, Adel, the pragmatic half of the couple, went to the kitchen. She touched Itchale lightly on his shoulder so as not to startle him and whispered to him gently, "Go wash your face. We have cried enough. I'll make us something to eat."

He got up and kissed her on the cheek, grateful that she knew just the right thing to say and do. "Adel, we have nothing left here. We need to get going."

*Now he is urging me to go. The times have changed,* she thought.

They ate the bread and drank the milk but packed the sausage for later use. They were not going to eat a sausage made of pork or drink it with the milk. Although not religious, they would not break Jewish religious laws out of respect for their dead families,

and especially not in Zelda's home. It would be almost sacrilegious to do so. They saw the packet of zloty and gratefully, packed that too, with the sausage.

"Another decent man," said Adel.

"A 'mensch' (a person of integrity and honor)," added Itchale.

They had to go far away from Poland and from their memories.

It was time to go to the Jewish land they had heard of— Palestine. *But where was it? And how should they get there?*

They walked out, one foot in front of the other, and never looked back.

Szczecin was a German city that became part of Poland after the war. And from that city, Jews left for Palestine, they were told.

So they decided to go to Szczecin. They took a train and a bus and headed to Szczecin.

Although grief became an integral part of their lives, Adel was pregnant again. Life was still stronger than death.

# 33
# A New Child is Born

They could tell by the looks and behavior of Jews they met in Szczecin which hell each had survived. Whether it was the Russian prisons, the gulags, or the Nazi death camps.

The worst were the death camp survivors. Their eyes were hollow. Some looked like the living dead. Many of them were not communicative at all. Their bodies were in this world, while their souls burned in the crematoriums.

Adel and Itchale rented an apartment from an old Baba Yaga, who hated the sight of the pregnant woman. However, she liked the money they paid her in advance.

"Jews," she hissed. "I can smell them. They don't fool me."

The one-bedroom apartment was near the shipyard, in a suburb of Szczecin, on the second floor of Dabrowki Street, number three.

Only a year earlier in this German city, the headquarters of the notorious Nazi SS had existed.

The building on Dabrowki Street looked as if it had been bombarded by the Allied forces only yesterday. The walls were damaged by shells and fire. And the surroundings looked frozen in time. Itchale found a job in the shipyard right away.

A few days after they had settled, Adel went into labor.

"Let me take you to the hospital," begged Itchale.

"No. I will not go to a German hospital."

"It is Polish now," said Itchale.

*What has gotten into her?* he wondered.

"Don't be foolish, you need help. I cannot deliver the baby." Adel did not budge.

"Didn't you hear about the pogroms?" she asked.

Although it was after the war, Jews were still killed in the streets and in organized massacres, "pogroms," in Poland, Russia, Ukraine, and in other places in Europe. Those murdered had survived the gulags, the ghettos, and death camps but not their neighbors.

With the help of a midwife, Adel gave birth, at home, to a baby girl.

Both parents were overjoyed. The baby seemed healthy. She demanded food.

"This is a good sign," said Adel.

But unfortunately, she had nothing to give. "My milk, like my tears, is dry."

Itchale had to take his wife and daughter to the hospital to get help. Because of the chaotic times, the registration process of the newborn's birth did not go smoothly. The father reported to the registrar one birth date and the mother a different one. The clerk heard and documented a third date altogether.

"Shouldn't we correct the date?" he asked.

Adel, who did not want to waste more time standing in the registration line in the city hall, said to the concerned father, "What difference does it make whether it says June or July? What's important is that she was born, not when."

What choice did he have but to agree?

"Go argue with her logic," he mumbled, smiling.

Besides, he had more important tasks to do than to stand in line to register a baby.

After several months in Szczecin, Adel, who never forgot they were only visitors, not settlers in town, was ready to go on.

She did not want to stay in Poland any longer for the same reasons she did not want to stay in Russia. She wanted "to live among Jews."

There was an active Jewish organization in Szczecin called "Habricha." Someone at the organization told them if they were determined to leave for Palestine, they had to go first to a displaced persons camp near a German town called Hofgeismar.

# 34
# A Family in Transition

About five hundred kilometers from Szczecin was the town of Hofgeismar and the camp named after it. Both were in Germany in the American Occupation Zone.

The United Nations with the United States had set up a camp for survivors. They then transported survivors to countries that agreed to accept them.

Adel and Itchale packed the few material belongings they had. And although it was still summer, Adel, who wanted to protect the baby from the cold night, dressed her up with as many clothes as she could put on. The baby almost suffocated but was too young to protest.

Itchale took one look at the baby and burst out laughing hysterically. "What have you done to her? She looks like a mummy!"

That was the second time Adel had heard him laugh since their son's death. *Thank God, that's a good sign*, she thought.

After many hours on a bus, the small family arrived at the camp, in the American Occupied Zone of Germany.

After tedious registration by American and United Nations representatives, they received a barrack and the next day were assigned for work.

Itchale, who wanted to get a better paying job, found work outside the camp in Hofgeismar. Adel worked at the camp with children, so she could keep her child with her all the time. The baby started walking in the camp. The camp was crowded with survivors of gulags and concentration camps from all over Europe. Newcomers arrived every day. But there was enough food and, considering the times, they were treated well. They stayed in the camp less than a year when one day they heard about a transport leaving to the nearest port. They embarked on a ship that would take them to Palestine.

# ON THE ROUTE TO PALESTINE-ISRAEL

# 35
# Captured

It was supposed to be a smooth journey. It was not.

From November 26, 1947—the day they left the camp—and during their entire journey to "the Promised Land," they were faced with more challenges.

The train, which left from Germany to take them to a port, was full of survivors like Itchale and Adel. When they were in the Mediterranean Sea, the ship was captured by the British army.

Palestine was still ruled by England. The British, who had no interest in allowing the Jewish population to grow, used all means to prevent the arrival of Jewish Holocaust survivors to Palestine.

The passengers were taken off the ship and, to their horror, transported to a detention camp in Marseille, France.

The camp, like most refugee camps, was crowded, chaotic, and filthy. It was surrounded by high fences and gates, with people from Europe and even North Africa, speaking dozens of languages.

It was not a melting pot of people helping one another but rather a boiling pot of people quarreling and arguing all day and about everything.

No wonder. They were all wounded by the war. Incapable of helping themselves and, needless to say, incapable of helping someone else. No country wanted them, and there was no comfort or assurance they'd make it to Palestine. Most of them did not even know where Palestine was. But it did not make any difference. They wanted to live where they would not be persecuted because they were Jewish. They needed to feel safe again.

Ironically enough, the safe place was Palestine—a disputed territory at that time.

# AN END AND A NEW BEGINNING

# 36
# In Israel

After several months, they were finally released from the camp. They were put on a ship—Negba—and arrived in Palestine in 1948—right at the end of the Israeli War of Independence.

Unbeknownst to the survivors, by the time they were released from the detention camp, the British had withdrawn from Palestine, the State of Israel was declared, and following the declaration of the state, the Arab countries surrounding Israel declared war on the new state, and the Israeli War of Independence broke out.

They had escaped one fire to arrive in another one. But now they were free people in a new homeland.

On March 22, 1966, eighteen years after their arrival in Israel, Itchale died of a heart attack. He was almost forty-nine years old. Three years later, Adel remarried. She was widowed again years later.

Adel lived through the death of Gili, her only granddaughter. But she lived to enjoy grandsons, especially her first born grandson—Shai, who was about to become a father.

Adel passed away at age eighty-six on October 27, 2003, only eighteen days before Jessica—her first great-granddaughter—was born. While Adel did not live to see Jessica, she felt her heartbeat when she was still in her mother's womb.

Adel's second great-granddaughter—Mika—bears resemblance to her.

Adel resigned herself to the unavoidable with a clear mind. She opened her eyes to another horizon—to her next journey.

# EPILOGUE

I am Adel's daughter. Itchale is my father. I am the one who listened to their hearts as long as I can remember. This is their story.

I tried to be a listener, even an interviewer, at times, a respectful interpreter of her stories. Never a judge. However, I am also a professional psychologist and a researcher. As such, I cannot listen without digging for underlying causes of thoughts, feelings, actions, and further "investigation."

Thirteen years after my mother's death, and decades after my father's, I embarked on a journey of discovery through research and travel, following my parents', but especially my mother's, stories.

I promised her "to tell."

The result is a story based on formal and non-formal documents. Although the story includes biographical facts, it is not a fully documented biography. I had to draw from other inspirational resources, such as my memories of actual conversations with my parents, especially with my mother; conversations with other relatives; Adel's diary; thorough research in Israeli, Polish, German, and other archives, documents, and books; and extensive travel across Russia and Poland. To places I heard about and memorized during my parents' entire lives. Nevertheless, my research was faced with difficulties in validating some details of my mother's story, due to selective memory, perception, interpretation, and knowledge of historical events and the subjective perception of time or her "psychological time" as compared to the objective measurement of time, or the universal—chronological time.

Many years ago, it was spring and the weather enticed us to be outdoors. I came from afar to visit my ailing mother. She lived in Israel, and I in the United States.

I was her pride and joy, "my daughter the professor, my best friend" as she introduced me to a passing neighbor. We took a gentle walk, arm in arm, around the block, as far as her health enabled her to walk. We sat down in the neighborhood park, on a deserted bench that had known better days. She sat straight. "Disciplined." Ready to talk. Willing to answer my questions. We had been waiting for these precious visits. The distant look in her eyes told me she is "there"—immersed in her past, flooded by memories. I loved listening to her stories of past and present. She told them in Yiddish blended with Hebrew. Her most horrific stories were told, mostly, in a calm and steady voice, but her eyes often filled with tears. I watched her. My heart went out to her. I wanted to fix her life and magically bring her loved ones back from the dead, my daughter Gili too.

# CONTEMPLATIONS

She said, "I'm a simple woman. What do I know? I just listened to my heart."

I listened too.

When she said, "What choice did I have?" she meant, "I had no choice but to listen to my heart." Her heart's choice was the right choice, with the right purpose.

I listened to her in amazement.

That unwanted child became a woman of values: civility, decency, integrity, kindness, devotion, and compassion for others with a tenacity and zest for life—a stubbornness to live.

She developed durable beliefs—in personal destiny and in the transcendental power of love.

Her upbringing bred tenacity, resilience, and an ability to adjust to new situations. All came into fruition when her husband disappeared.

In fact, Adel had no say or control over her life until she was about twenty years old when she got married and she and her husband felt safe with each other.

However, the disappearance of her husband—her bashert—was the loss to which she could not react passively. The young woman who reclaimed control over her life was transformed into a formidable woman.

*In* order to survive, she did not allow herself to dwell on the painful past. Rather, she focused on the present and looked forward with intention.

"I never looked back, only forward," she said. From that moment, she shuffled her cards again and again.

Adel, who attested that she "never looked back"—a self-testimony, which was meant to be both an example, a scolding and advice—in my life journey—did in fact look back. She had an urgent need to tell and retell her story.

When I asked her, "Why are you telling me?"

She answered, "Your generation would not believe such atrocities happened to us (Jews). You have to remember and tell others."

I remember and I tell.

"What was the meaning of your journey?" I asked her.

"Finding my husband. I had hoped he was alive, of course. But, regardless, I had to find out what happened to him. Whether he searched for me or waited for me was less important. However, in time, my journey took on a meaning of its own. I felt alive when I could walk. But I was alive because I searched for my bashert. And finding him made my life worth living."

I had so many questions left, but one in particular bothered me.

"Was it still love that drove you so relentlessly to keep searching for him?"

"Love at first, for sure," she said. "Was it still love if it was marred by doubts? Did he love me as much as I loved him? Would he have searched for me if it were me who was abducted? Was he waiting for me? Or did he 'let go' of me? Those were toxic questions. Painful, with no answer. I stopped asking myself love questions. I had to trust the feelings I remembered we had for each other since we were twelve years old. Our history together and our commitment to each other when we got married. So, yes, mein tochter (my daughter), I always loved him. And I'll love him till my last breath."

# CLOSURE

During my search, I recognized similarities to my parents, not only in the tangible but also in my resilience and drive.

A circle of sort was closed when I got both death certificates. Adel and Itchale, who during the war were refugees who risked their lives with no documents or certificates, could rest in peace now.

In her journey, my mother searched for a future.

In my journey, I searched for a past and found a future.

And I fell in love with my parents—all over again.

# APPENDICES

# CONCEPTS AND DEFINITIONS
## Adel's and Itchale's Journeys

## —A—

**Adel(a)'s Memoir-Diary:** During several weeks in 2002, my mother wrote selected memories in a notebook. She filled up thirty-eight pages written almost without any punctuation marks. She wrote in a blend of Yiddish and Hebrew, using the Polish alphabet because she could not write in Yiddish although she spoke the language. See sample of Adel's diary pages on the next page.

**Almaty, Kazakhstan:** This is the largest, most developed, and most ethnically and culturally diverse city in Kazakhstan. Due to the relocation of workers and industries from European areas of the Soviet Union during World War II, the city has a high proportion of ethnic Russians and Ukrainians.

**Asbest, the Urals, Russia:** A town in Sverdlovsk Oblast, Russia, which is located on the Bolshoy Reft River on the eastern slopes of the Ural Mountains seventy kilometers northeast of Yekaterinburg (Sverdlovsk). The town is named for its asbestos industry.

## —B—

**Baba Yaga:** In Slavic folklore, a deformed and/or ferocious-looking witch.

**Bashert:** (Yiddish) A soulmate; an ideal or predestined marriage partner.

**Belzec, Poland:** An extermination death camp within the Lublin District about sixty-five kilometers from Izbica. It was built in the early 1940s by the Nazis for the purpose of eliminating the Polish Jewry as part of their Final Solution plan.

**Taken from Adel's Diary**

**Taken from Adel's Diary**

# —E—

**Escape of Polish Jews to Russia:** During the last months of 1939 and the beginning of 1940, even before the Russian Red Army and the Nazis invaded Poland, Polish Jews were not locked inside ghettos and were "encouraged" to escape Poland and settle in Russia. However, the Russians did not welcome those Polish refugees. Hundreds of thousands were captured, imprisoned, and sent to labor camps in Siberia or to remote kolkhozes, villages in European and Asian Russia. The refugees had to live not only under torturous conditions but also had to undergo reeducation in the Communist doctrine. They were constantly under the surveillance of the NKVD.

# —G—

**Gulag, USSR:** (Russian) This is an acronym for "main administration of the camps," the government agency that administered the main Soviet forced labor camp systems during the Stalin era from the 1930s until the 1950s. Forced labor camps continued to function outside of the agency until the late 1980s. The first such camps were created in 1918 and the term is widely used to describe any forced labor camp in the USSR. The gulag is recognized as a major instrument of political repression in the Soviet Union. While the camps housed a wide range of convicts, from petty criminals to political prisoners, large numbers of Jews were kidnapped and imprisoned for no other reason than being refugees with no identification documents.

# —H—

**Hofgeismar Displaced Persons (DPs) Camp, Germany:** Located about 30 km north of Kassel in the American Occupied Zone, it maintained a hospital and a number of schools. The living conditions were relatively good, although the camp was overcrowded. The DPs lived in barracks with two or three families living in one room. UNRRA (the United Nations Relief and Rehabilitation) and the United States Army set up the camp in 1945 for Jewish refugees and those liberated from the concentration camps.

**Holocaust:** Also referred to as the Shoah. A genocide in which about 6 million out of 9.5 million European Jews alive at that time (60 percent of the world's Jews) were murdered by Adolf Hitler's Nazi Germany and the World War II collaborators with the Nazis. The Holocaust began in January 1933 when Hitler came to power and technically ended on May 8, 1945 (VE Day). Over 1.1 million children were murdered by the Nazis during the Holocaust.

# —I—

**Irkutsk, Siberia, Russia:** A city situated in a landscape of rolling hills within the thick taiga that is typical to Eastern Siberia. Irkutsk has a borderline subarctic climate. The city is an administrative center and one of the largest cities in Siberia. During the Communist years, the industrialization of Irkutsk, and Siberia in general, was heavily encouraged. The city proper lies on the Angara River, a tributary of the Yenisei, seventy-two kilometers below its outflow from Lake Baikal.

**Izbica, Poland:** A small town nestled in the valley of the Wieprz River in the Krasnystaw County in southeastern Poland. It lies approximately thirteen kilometers south of Krasnystaw and fifty-nine kilometers southeast of the regional capital, Lublin. Today, it has a population of 1,933.

Izbica was first mentioned in a church document from 1419 and became a town in 1750, granted location privileges by Augustus III of Poland, including the right of a Jewish settlement. A notable center of trade and commerce, the town became a shtetl inhabited almost entirely by Polish Jews. After the partitions of Poland in 1772, Izbica was annexed by Austria-Hungary and then purchased back from the Austrian government in 1808.

Following the Congress of Vienna in June 1815, Izbica joined the Russian-controlled Congress Poland. The town was consumed by fire in 1825. In 1827, it had 51 houses and 407 inhabitants, all of them Jewish. By 1860, the population tripled to 1,450 Jews.

In the nineteenth century, Izbica was probably the most unusual of Jewish shtetls in Poland. It was called "The Jewish Capital," perhaps because the majority of the population was Jewish and the town was a notable center of Hasidic Judaism—the Hasidic dynasty of Ishbitz.

In the twentieth century, following Poland's return to independence in the aftermath of World War I, the town grew significantly. Streets were paved and the marketplace rebuilt. According to the 1921 census, Izbica had 3,085 inhabitants including 2,862 Jews, but by 1939, the total number grew to roughly 6,000 with 5,098 Jews. Following the German and Soviet invasion of Poland in 1939 during the opening stages of World War II, the town was overrun by the Nazis. In the spring of 1941, in preparation for the attack on the Soviet lines in Eastern Poland, the German military storage facilities were set up in Izbica.

The Izbica ghetto was also set up by the Nazis. The first mass deportation of ghetto inmates to the Belzec extermination camp took place in mid-March 1942, conducted by the Germans with the aid of Ukrainians. The ghetto served as a transfer point to the extermination camps in Belzec and Sobibor for foreign Jews deported from Germany, Austria, Czechoslovakia, and western Poland. Of all the Jews of Izbica (over 90 percent of its pre-war population), only fourteen survived the Holocaust.

**The Izbica ghetto:** Created by Nazi Germany in Izbica in occupied Poland during World War II, it served as a transfer point for deportation of Jews from Poland, Germany, Austria, and Czechoslovakia to Belzec and Sobibor extermination camps. The ghetto was created in 1941, although the first transports of Jews from the German Reich started arriving there as early as 1940. Izbica was the largest transit ghetto in the Lublin Reservation with a death rate almost equal to that of the Warsaw ghetto.

## —J—

**Jews in Russian Asia/Central Asia:** The history of Jews in Central Asia dates back centuries, where Jews have lived in countries including Kyrgyzstan, Kazakhstan, Mongolia, Uzbekistan, and Tajikistan.

**Jews in Kazakhstan:** Most Kazakh Jews are Ashkenazi and speak Russian. General Secretary Joseph Stalin forcibly moved thousands of Jews from other parts of the Soviet Union to the Kazakh SSR. During the Holocaust, eight thousand Jews fled to Kazakhstan. The Jewish population grew significantly in the 1930s and 1940s by migration from the former Pale of Settlement and from mass evacuation in 1941–42 when over one hundred thousand Jews from the European part of the USSR were brought to Kazakhstan.

## —K—

**Kolkhoz, USSR:** (Russian) A form of a commune, a collective farm in the Soviet Union since the revolution of 1917. An antithesis to individual or family farms. In the Stalin period, individual farmers were forced to give up their farms and join a kolkhoz.

# —L—

**Lake Baikal, Russia:** The largest freshwater lake in the world with an average depth of 744.4 meters, it contains roughly 20 percent of the world's surface fresh water.

The body of water is also known as the "Baikal Sea" and the "Pearl of Siberia." At 1,642 meters, Lake Baikal is the deepest and among the clearest lakes in the world. At more than twenty-five million years old, Baikal is also the world's oldest lake. Baikal is home to more than seventeen hundred species of plants and animals, two-thirds of which can be found nowhere else in the world, and was declared a UNESCO World Heritage Site in 1996. It is also home to the Buryat people who follow the Tibetan Buddhist religion and reside on the eastern side of the lake rearing goat, camel, cattle, and sheep.

# —M—

**Majdanek, Poland:** A German extermination death camp on the outskirts of the city of Lublin, in southeast Poland, it was built by the Nazis in the early 1940s as part of their Final Solution plan to eliminate all Jews.

**Makhorka:** (Russian) A cigarette, rolled by hand and filled with cheap tobacco or another substance.

**Menschlichkeit:** (Yiddish, German) Compassion, humaneness.

**Mitzvah:** (Hebrew, Yiddish) A precept or commandment. Also, a good deed from religious duty.

**Mongolia:** Mongolia State is a landlocked unitary sovereign state in East Asia. It is sandwiched between China to the south and Russia to the north. While it does not share a border with Kazakhstan, Mongolia is separated from it by only 36.76 kilometers.

At 1,564,116 square kilometers, Mongolia is the eighteenth largest country in the world by land mass and has a population of around three million people. It is also the world's second-largest landlocked country behind Kazakhstan and the largest land-locked country that does not border a closed sea. The country contains very little arable land as much of its area is covered by grassy steppe with mountains to the north and west and the Gobi Desert to the south. Ulaanbaatar, the capital and largest city, is home to 40 to 45 percent of the country's population.

Approximately 97 percent of the population is nomadic or semi-nomadic; horse culture is still integral. The majority of its population are Buddhists. The non-religious population is the second-largest group. Islam is the dominant religion among ethnic Kazakhs. The majority of the state's citizens are of Mongol/Mongolian ethnicity, although Kazakhs, Tuvans, and other minorities also live in the country, especially in the west.

## —N—

**NKVD (Russia):** The People's Commissariat for Internal Affairs or Stalin's secret police, the NKVD, is the feared Russian law enforcement agency of the whole Soviet Union that executed the will of the All-Union Communist Party.

## —P—

**Partisan(s):** A resistance fighter. A member of an armed group formed to fight secretly against an occupying force in parts of Eastern Europe in World War II, such as in Russia and other enemy-occupied countries as Italy, France, and Yugoslavia. Jewish partisans were fighters in irregular military groups participating in the Jewish resistance movement against Nazi Germany and its collaborators during World War II.

A number of Jewish partisan groups operated across Nazi-occupied Europe. Some were made up of a few escapees from the Jewish ghettos or concentration camps, while others numbered in the hundreds and included women and children. They were most numerous in Eastern Europe, but groups also existed in occupied France and Belgium where they worked with the local resistance. Many individual Jewish fighters took part in other partisan movements in other occupied countries. In all, the Jewish partisans numbered between twenty and thirty thousand.

**Pogrom(s):** A violent riot aimed at the massacre or persecution of an ethnic or religious group, particularly one aimed at Jews. The first anti-Jews pogrom was in Odessa, Russia, in 1821. The last pogrom was on July 4, 1946, in Kielce, Poland.

**Poland during World War I (1916–18):** While Poland did not exist as an independent state during World War I, its geographical position between the fighting powers meant that much fighting and terrific human and material losses occurred on the Polish lands between

1914 and 1918. When World War I started, the Polish territory split during partitions between Austria-Hungary (all of Eastern Poland, including Izbica), the German Empire, and the Russian Empire, and it became the scene of much of the operations of the Eastern Front of World War I. In the aftermath of the war, following the collapse of the Russian, German, and Austro-Hungarian Empires, Poland became an independent republic.

**Poland between WWI and WWII (1918–39):** The history of interwar Poland comprises the period from the re-creation of the independent Polish state in 1918 until the joint invasion of Poland by Nazi Germany and the Soviet Union in 1939 at the onset of World War II. The two decades of Poland's sovereignty between the World Wars are known as the interbellum (interwar period).

## —S—

**Shtetl:** (Yiddish) A small Jewish town or village in Eastern Europe.

**Sobibor, Poland:** A German death camp located in the eastern part of the Lublin District of Poland. The camp was five kilometers from the Bug River which today forms the border between Poland and the Ukraine. Sobibor was the second death camp built in the early 1940s, on similar lines to Belzec, incorporating the lessons learned from the first death camp to be constructed.

**Szczecin (Polish/Stettin), (Swedish and German):** A city in the northwest of the Republic of Poland. It is the capital city of the West Pomeranian Voivodeship in Poland. Located on the Oder river, near the Baltic Sea, it is a major seaport. The city's recorded history began in the eighth century. Until 1720, it was controlled by Sweden. In 1870, it was part of the German Empire. In the late nineteenth century, Stettin became an industrial center and served as a major port for Berlin. During the Nazi era, it was part of Germany, and the third-largest city after Berlin and Hamburg. In 1940, the Jews of Stettin were deported to the Lublin Reservation. In 1944, Allied air raids and heavy fighting between the German and Soviet armies destroyed 65 percent of Stettin's buildings. In 1945, most of the German population fled the city.

By the end of WWII, Stettin's status was in doubt, and the Soviet occupation authorities first appointed officials from the city's pre-war, almost entirely German, population. But in July 1945, Polish authorities were permitted to take power. Stettin was transferred to Poland and renamed Szczecin.

In 1945 and 1946, the city was the starting point of the northern route used by the Jewish underground organization "Bricha" to channel Jewish Displaced Persons (DPs) from Central and Eastern Europe to the American Occupation Zone.

## —T—

**Talmud:** (Hebrew) The body of Jewish civil and ceremonial law and legend comprising the Mishnah and the Gemara. There are two versions of the Talmud: the Babylonian AD Talmud that dates from the fifth century and the earlier Jerusalem Talmud.

**Taiga, Siberia, Russia:** Also known as boreal forest or snow forest, the taiga is a biome characterized by coniferous forests consisting mostly of pines, spruces, and larches.

The taiga is the world's largest biome apart from the oceans. Much of Russia, from Karelia in the west to the Pacific Ocean (including much of Siberia) and areas of northern Kazakhstan and northern Mongolia, are covered with the taiga.

**Tashkent, Uzbekistan:** Literally "Stone City," Tashkent is the capital and largest city of Uzbekistan. Due to its position in Central Asia, Tashkent came under Sogdian and Turkic influence early in its history before Islam became prominent in eighth century AD. After its destruction by Genghis Khan in 1219, the city was rebuilt and profited from the Silk Road. In 1865, it was conquered by the Russian Empire and, in Soviet times, witnessed major growth and demographic changes due to forced deportations from throughout the Soviet Union. Today, as the capital of an independent Uzbekistan, Tashkent retains a multiethnic population with ethnic Uzbeks as the majority.

**The Trans-Siberian Train (The Trans-Siberian Railway), Russia:** A network of railways connecting Moscow with the Russian Far East, the Trans-Siberian train, with a length of 9,289 kilometers, is the longest railway line in the world. There are connecting branch lines into Mongolia, China, and North Korea. It has connected Moscow with Vladivostok since 1916 and is still being expanded.

It was built between 1891 and 1916 under the supervision of Russian government ministers personally appointed by Tsar Alexander III and his son, the Tsarevich Nicholas

(later Tsar Nicholas II). The railway is often associated with the main transcontinental Russian line connecting hundreds of large and small cities of the European and Asian parts of Russia. It spans a record eight time zones.

The Trans-Siberian route starts in Moscow and terminates in Vladivostok (Far East, the shore of Pacific Ocean).

## —U—

**Ulaanbaatar, Mongolia:** Ulaanbaatar, formerly anglicized as Ulan Bator (Mongolian: Ulananbaatur, literally "Red Hero"), is Mongolia's capital and largest city. A municipality,

the city is not part of any province, and its population as of 2014 was over 1.3 million, almost half of the country's total population.

Located in north central Mongolia, the municipality lies at an elevation of about thirteen hundred meters in a valley on the Tuul River. It is the country's cultural, industrial, and financial heart, the center of Mongolia's road network and connected by rail to both the Trans-Siberian Railway in Russia and the Chinese railway system.

**Ulan-Ude, Buryatia, Russia (Buryat: Ulaan** Üde): The capital city of the Republic of Buryatia, Russia, it is located about a hundred kilometers southeast of Lake Baikal on the Uda River at its confluence with the Selenga. The third-largest city in eastern Siberia by population, the ethnic makeup of the city consists of Russians, Buryats, Ukrainians, Tatars, and others. The city is the center of Tibetan Buddhism in Russia.

## —V—

**Vladivostok, Russia (Russian. Literally, ruler of the east):** This city is the administrative center of Primorsky Krai, Russia, located at the head of the Golden Horn Bay, not far from Russia's borders with China and North Korea, on the "edge" of Russia's Far East. The city is the home port of the Russian Pacific Fleet and the largest Russian port on the Pacific Ocean. After the October Revolution, the Bolsheviks took control of Vladivostok and the Trans-Siberian Railway in its entirety. As the main naval base of the Soviet Pacific Fleet, Vladivostok was officially closed to foreigners during the Soviet years.

## —W—

**World War I (WWI ):** Known as the First World War, the Great War, or the War to End All Wars, it was a global war originating in Europe lasting from July 28, 1914, to November 11, 1918, (four years, three months, and two weeks). The war spanned Europe, Africa, the Middle East, the Pacific Islands, China, Indian Ocean, and South and North Africa.

Over nine million combatants and seven million civilians died as a result of the war, including the victims of a number of genocides.

It was one of the deadliest conflicts in history and paved the way for major political changes, including revolutions in many of the nations involved. The result was the fall of the German, Russian, Ottoman, and Austro-Hungarian Empires and the formation of new countries in Europe (including Poland) and in the Middle East.

**World War II (WWII):** Known as the Second World War. It started on September 1, 1939, and ended on September 2, 1945 (six years and one day).

The war started with the invasion of Poland by Nazi Germany. It was a global war, although related conflicts began earlier. It involved the vast majority of the world's countries—including all of the great powers—eventually forming two opposing military alliances: the Allies (mainly Russia and the United States) and the Axis (Nazi Germany, Japan, and Italy). It was the most widespread war in history and directly involved more than one hundred million people from over thirty countries. Marked by mass deaths of civilians, including the Holocaust in which approximately eleven million people were killed. Of them, six million were Jews, among them one million children—a third of all the Jews in the world at that time. It resulted

in an estimated fifty to eighty-five million fatalities (including those of the atomic bombing of Hiroshima and Nagasaki). These deaths made World War II the deadliest conflict in human history.

# —Y—

**Yarmulke:** A skullcap worn by religious Jews.

# —Z—

**Zima, Siberia, Russia:** A town in Irkutsk Oblast, Russia, it is located at the point where the Trans-Siberian Railway crosses the Oka River.

The local climate is extremely continental; air temperature varies between -45 °C (-49 °F) in winter to +40 °C (104 °F) in summer.

The town is the birthplace of Yevgeny Yevtushenko, the renowned Russian poet, the author of the poems "Zima Station" and "Babi Yar."